CW01650906

Nelson Music

2

Mary Edwards   Lis Fletcher

Nelson

Lis Fletcher is a music consultant. She provides professional development for music teachers and also works with children in schools. Lis was a member of the music advisory team for Gloucestershire.

Mary Edwards is the music advisory teacher for Avon. She is responsible for the professional development programme in music, which involves working with teachers and children in schools.

Contents

Introduction

Nelson Music is a resource for non-specialist music teachers that provides complete coverage of curriculum-based music in primary schools.

The scheme has three stages:
Nelson Music 1 (ages 4 – 7)
Nelson Music 2 (ages 7 – 9)
Nelson Music 3 (ages 9 – 12)

Each stage has a teacher's book with six accompanying cassettes or three compact discs. The teacher's book contains a programme of activities which provide gradual progression. It also includes:

- advice on classroom management e.g. strategies for organising the classroom, use of instruments, management of group work
- assessment strategies and a photocopiable assessment sheet
- cross-curricular links
- a glossary of musical terms
- a visual glossary of musical instruments
- photocopiable flashcards
- sheet music for the songs in the scheme

The cassettes and compact discs contain identical material. They provide all the songs and listening extracts required for the scheme. These occur in broadly the same order as they are referred to in the teacher's book.

How does Nelson Music 2 work?

The teacher's book is divided into two parts:

Units 1, 2 and 3 contain work for children aged 7 – 8 (green pages).

Units 4, 5 and 6 contain work for children aged 8 – 9 (orange pages).

Within each unit there are a series of short activities. Each activity focuses on the musical elements. The activities are followed by more extended blocks of work which consolidate and integrate the skills and knowledge already developed.

Each of the units 1 to 6 begin with activities, to introduce a key musical element. These are followed by an extended block of work. This in turn is divided into four **sections** which are expected to last for at least an hour:

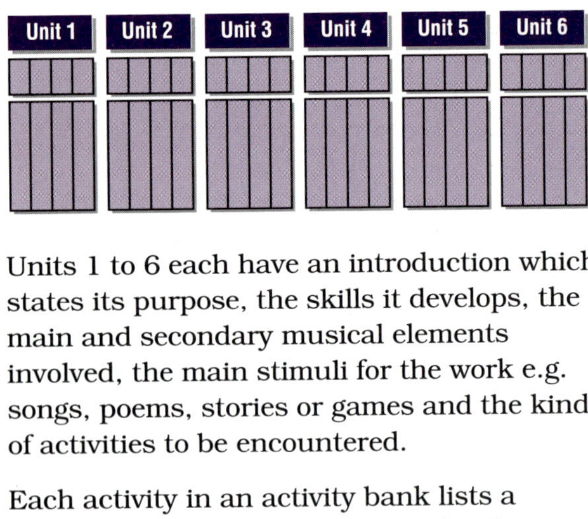

Units 1 to 6 each have an introduction which states its purpose, the skills it develops, the main and secondary musical elements involved, the main stimuli for the work e.g. songs, poems, stories or games and the kinds of activities to be encountered.

Each activity in an activity bank lists a purpose, resources and time guide. If an activity takes place somewhere other than the classroom, this is also indicated.

How do I use Nelson Music 2?

The scheme provides for a gradual progression and is designed to be taught sequentially. The activities at the beginning of the unit are intended to be taught for short periods of time, more than once, to gradually develop and reinforce learning. Activities can be taught whenever you have a few minutes to spare – first thing in the morning, before or after break, before the end of the school day. Alternatively, several activities could be combined into a more extended lesson.

Each section lasts for at least an hour. The time required will vary substantially from classroom to classroom. Sections may be spread across two or three lessons, if convenient.

A time guide is provided for each activity and each section. This is to assist you in planning, and is not intended to be prescriptive. Inevitably, certain pieces of work will take longer or shorter than suggested, depending on your circumstances.

What teaching and learning approaches are used?

This scheme assumes that the most effective way for children to gain an understanding of music is through opportunities to explore, recognise and respond to the musical elements of pitch, duration, dynamics, tempo, timbre, texture and structure.

At this stage, children will continue to need structured opportunities to build up a vocabulary of sounds. Within this structured approach, there is ample opportunity for individual creative responses. Children will learn most effectively if they discuss and question what they are hearing and doing. Many activities encourage this.

There is a mixture of teacher-led, whole-class activities, and work for small groups and pairs, but allowing for a good degree of teacher control. A large number of activities require children to sit in a circle. This has a reassuring effect, and it also means that you can see everyone and they can see you.

Musical games are an important feature of **Nelson Music** – they are an effective and highly enjoyable way of building musical skills. They allow you to manage activities in a non-threatening way and, if children do something incorrectly, you can try and help them find the correct answer without embarrassing them. Some strategies are

suggested within the text. Games should be repeated several times, in order to reinforce the musical skill involved, to give the children confidence and familiarity with the activity, and to allow them the opportunity to play several different instruments.

If you find that some children do not join in an activity, there is no need to force them to do so, unless they are being obviously disruptive. Quite often, children who appear not to be participating will be quietly absorbing information.

How does Nelson Music 2 cover the National Curriculum?

Nelson Music 2 provides comprehensive coverage of the revised National Curriculum (1994) for music for years 3 and 4 of

Key Stage Two. The entire music order is covered at a level that is appropriate for children aged 7 to 9.

- Each of units 1 to 6 focuses on understanding a particular musical element combined with developing appropriate skills. The unit introductions show which elements and general programme of study items are going to be focused on in that unit. The activity bank at the beginning of the unit focuses on the element, and the four sections which follow extend this work and combine it with the skills specified in the general programme of study.
- The chart on page 10 shows at a glance how Nelson Music 2 correlates to the requirements of the National Curriculum.

How does Nelson Music 2 cover the curricular requirements for Northern Ireland and Scotland?

The charts on pages 12–15 illustrate at a glance how Nelson Music 2 correlates to the Curriculum Orders for Northern Ireland and the 5–14 Guidelines for Scotland.

What assessment strategies are used?

- Opportunities for assessment are identified wherever appropriate in units 1 to 6 in the form of **observation points**. These help teachers to develop their ability to assess children's musical development.
- At the conclusion of each unit is an **end-of-unit checkpoint** which relates to the purpose of the unit.
- A photocopiable **assessment sheet** (page 142) can be used to record a child's progress in relation to the requirements of the National Curriculum. This will provide a record of each child's development over Years 3 and 4 .

How does Nelson Music fit into the whole curriculum?

Music offers a great deal of scope for meaningful links with other areas of the curriculum. Certain of these links have been highlighted, throughout the book, under the heading **cross-curricular links.** (A list of these cross-curricular activities is on page 139.)

However, in Nelson Music there are many more cross-curricular activities, as well as opportunities for the teacher to draw further cross-curricular links where they wish to do so.

How does Nelson Music provide access to the curriculum for all children?

The activities have been designed to take into account children's differences, in terms of race, gender, class or disability. Music for listening and singing has been selected from a range of countries and musical traditions. You may wish to extend this by introducing additional material which reflects the cultures of particular children in the school. See below for advice on addressing the requirements of children with special educational needs.

Children with special educational needs

All children are different and their different needs require consideration. This is especially true of children with special educational needs. Each child needs to be thought about carefully – try to plan ahead so that everyone can participate to the best of their ability.

Children with weak motor skills could use large instruments or instruments that make less precise sound patterns, e.g. shaking instruments.

Children with a hearing impairment could be given instruments through which they can feel a vibration, e.g. drums, bass chime bars, cymbals. Make sure that they can see you clearly, and when clapping a beat, make it very visual.

Visually impaired children should sit close to anyone making signals – there should not be a light behind the person they need to see.

If a child struggles to articulate words clearly, then encourage them to participate to the best of their ability. If they prefer not to sing, encourage them to play an instrument or use body percussion.

What additional resources are required?

All resources required are listed at the start of each activity or section. A tape recorder or a compact disc player is necessary.

A list of instruments that you need in order to involve all children is shown below.

Instruments you will need

Wooden:
- wood-block *
- two-tone wood-block
- claves *
- wooden agogo *
- gato drum/slit drum
- finger castanets *

Metal:
- sleigh bells *
- triangle (large)
- indian bells *
- cymbal and beater *
- pop jingle

Skin:
- tambour *
- tambourine *
- drums
- bongo drums

Shakers and scrapers
- guiro *
- maracas *
- cabasa *
- multi-guiro
- tubo

Beaters
Try to have a variety of types, with soft, medium and hard heads.

Extras: exciting and different sounds
- rainmaker
- ocean drums
- vibra slap
- flexitone
- homemade instruments

You should also have a few instruments on which it is possible to demonstrate different levels of pitch, i.e. high and low sounds.

- wood or metal chime bars (chromatic) *
- xylophone (alto – including F# and B♭) *
- metallophone (alto – including F# and B♭)
- glockenspiel
- bass chime bars (C, D, G, A)
- hand chimes

Most other resources are everyday materials that should be easily available in classrooms.

What instruments are required?

A classroom should have a variety of untuned instruments, which can be played in different ways, for example hit, shaken or scraped as well as some instruments that provide a variety of kinds of sounds e.g. metal, wood or skin. One of each of the asterisked items is an adequate minimum supply. Other items are desirable additions to your collection, but not essential. (See pages 140–141 for a visual glossary of musical instruments.)

In total, try to have at least one instrument between two children, to facilitate pair work.

Managing instruments

Encourage children to handle instruments with care, as many of them are expensive, and some are relatively fragile. Children should know where the instruments are kept, and assist with putting them away.

- When you hand out instruments, do not allow the children to play them until you tell them to e.g. tell them to place the instruments on the floor in front of them and 'glue' their hands to their knees until you say the 'magic' word.
- If a child refuses to co-operate, take their instrument away for a while.
- At times you may want all the children to experiment for a *few seconds*. Have a predesignated symbol to tell them to stop. A silent, visual signal e.g. raising your arm, is often better than shouting or playing an instrument loudly.
- You may wish to restrict the number of instruments that you hand out (e.g. give one to every two or three children in a circle), especially in the early weeks of the course, until the children have learned to handle them in a disciplined way.

Where a limited number of instruments are being used, involve all the children in the activity in the following ways:

- Where appropriate, encourage children who do not have instruments to use voices or body percussion e.g. clap, pat or tap knees.
- Ask the children without instruments specific questions in order to focus their listening while the others play.
- Repeat the activity, allowing different children to have the instruments – try to ensure that everyone has a chance.

How to teach a song (using the cassettes/compact discs)

- Play the whole song through once – ask the children to listen carefully.
- Play it again and ask the children to keep the steady beat, using their bodies (hand clap, knee pat, etc.)
- If there are any difficult or unfamiliar words, teach the children what they mean and how to pronounce them.
- The next time the song is played, encourage the children to sing along with any lines or words that are repeated.
- Play the song again, and let them sing any other words or phrases they can remember.
- Play it again, for the children to join in. Observe whether they are doing the following, and implement the suggested strategies.

Are they singing the right words?
Go through the words without the music.

Are they singing with clear diction?
Speak the words clearly and ask the children to say them after you.

Are they shouting?
Encourage them to sing quietly first, then slightly louder until they reach the desired level of loudness.

Are they breathing in the correct place i.e. do the sentences make sense?
Read the sentences without sense to show how important it is to breathe at the right time.

Repeat the song as many times as you feel appropriate, encouraging the children to make improvements where necessary.

Symbols or graphic notations

Children should be encouraged to perform from symbols and also to use them to communicate musical ideas to others. There are many opportunities for this kind of work in the scheme. On some occasions it may not be appropriate to store children's compositions in a written format, but rather to tape them onto a cassette or video.

Musical language

Understanding and using musical language is an important means of developing musical knowledge and skills. The first time a musical term occurs in the text it is explained. Musical terms are also clearly explained in a glossary on page 143. There are two pages of clear colour photographs of classroom percussion instruments on pages138–139.

Understanding rhythm

When teachers are asked to clap a rhythm, it is often described in terms of long and short sounds e.g. long, short, short, long. A clap makes a short sound, but if you say the words long, short, short, long as you clap, then an obvious pattern is heard.

You will also find reference to a series of syllables that will help you and the children perform rhythm patterns (see **Glossary**, Time names, for a fuller explanation of this).

National Curriculum for

England and Wales

Key Stage 2 Programme of study

Throughout Nelson Music 2 opportunities exist for individual, pair, group and whole class work. Opportunities for the appropriate use of IT are also highlighted.

	Unit 1	Unit 2	Unit 3	Unit 4	Unit 5	Unit 6
2 Elements						
• pitch		●			●	○
• duration	●	○	○	○		○
• dynamics		○	○	●	○	○
• tempo		○				●
• timbre			●	○	○	○
• texture	○		●	○	○	
• structure	○	●			○	●
3 Repertoire						
• different times and cultures	◒	◒	◒	◒	◒	●
• composers and performers			○		○	○
4 Opportunities						
a control sounds						
• sing songs from memory, developing control of diction and musical elements, particularly phrasing	◒	○	○	◒	○	○
• play pieces and accompaniments, and perform musical patterns by ear and from notations	●	●		●	◒	○
b perform						
• sing songs, including songs and rounds in two parts, and play pieces which have several parts, developing the ability to listen to other performers	●	○	◒	○	○	●
• rehearse and present their own projects/ performances	○	●		○		

	Unit 1	Unit 2	Unit 3	Unit 4	Unit 5	Unit 6
c compose						
• improvise rhythmic and melodic ideas		●	○		●	●
• explore, create, select, combine and organise sounds in musical structures		●	●	○	●	○
d communicate						
• use sounds and structures to achieve an intended effect				◒		○
• refine and record their own compositions using notation(s) wherever appropriate		◒		◒	●	
e listen						
• identify the sounds made by a variety of instruments, individually and in combination		◒	◒	◒		
• identify how musical instruments and resources can be used to communicate a mood or effect	◒	○	●	●	◒	
• recognise ways in which the music reflects the time and place in which it is created	○		○			●
f respond						
• combine music from contrasting musical traditions and respond to differences in character and mood	○		●			●
• express ideas and opinions about music, developing a musical vocabulary and the ability to use musical knowledge to support views	◒	○	◒	◒	◒	◒

Key

○ visited

◒ explored

● main focus

Expressive Arts 5–14

Scottish Guidelines

OUTCOMES: using materials, techniques, skills and media

	Unit 1	Unit 2	Unit 3	Unit 4	Unit 5	Unit 6
STRANDS: investigating: exploring sound						
b explore sound quality and become familiar with the ways in which sounds are made and produced	○	◒	●	◒		○
c experiment with different combinations and qualities of sound to represent contrasting moods and effects		●	●			◒
STRANDS: using the voice						
b • show a greater ability to sing in tune with others	◒	○		○	◒	
• fit words to the melody where this is obvious	○	○		○	○	○
• control rhythm, speed and leaps in melody	◒	◒		○	●	●
c • sing together confidently in unison with some awareness of dynamics, phrasing and expression	◒	○		◒	○	○
• sustain a simple harmonic part	○	○	○			
STRANDS: using instruments						
b • play simple melodic and rhythm parts, sharing some control over speed and volume, and respond to simple signals of direction in performance	●	○		●	●	
c • display two-handed co-ordination in playing straightforward melodies and rhythms, sometimes using a form of written notation, paying attention to expression and contrasts in the music	○			◒	◒	○

Key

○ visited

◒ explored

● main focus

OUTCOMES: expressing feelings, ideas, thoughts and solutions

	Unit 1	Unit 2	Unit 3	Unit 4	Unit 5	Unit 6
STRANDS: creating and designing						
b • create simple sound pictures conveying an imaginative response to a stimulus and demonstrating an awareness of contrasts in music		●	●			●
• devise graphic symbols to represent the music			●		●	●
c • create sound pictures which convey mood and atmosphere, displaying imagination and some awareness of structure		●	●		◒	●
• devise a simplified form of notation to represent inventions visually		◒		◒	◒	
STRANDS: communicating and presenting						
a-e • work co-operatively in a group while music making or inventing, sharing a respect for the opinions of others – when and where appropriate, present and perform arrangements, songs, improvisations etc. to others	◒	●	◒	○	◒	

OUTCOMES: evaluating and appreciating

	Unit 1	Unit 2	Unit 3	Unit 4	Unit 5	Unit 6
STRANDS: observing, listening, reflecting, describing and responding						
b • describe the quality of environmental sounds in terms of source, volume, distance and location		○	○		○	
• discuss the characteristics of music with a clearly identifiable mood in terms of speed or volume	○	◒	◒	◒	○	●
• recognise the sounds of instruments which have a distinctive quality, e.g. bagpipe, trumpet, flute, piano or guitar		◒	○	○		◒
c • recognise the sounds of such obvious groupings as pipe band, orchestra, rock group, choir	○		○			◒
• demonstrate aural retention through playing phrases from familiar tunes by ear	○			○		
• give opinions of own music making and that of others and accept and offer suggestions for improvement		○	◒			◒

Music curriculum orders

Northern Ireland

Attainment Target 1: making music

SoA's

	Unit 1	Unit 2	Unit 3	Unit 4	Unit 5	Unit 6
Level 2						
a select sounds in response to a stimulus		●	○		○	●
b invent symbols to represent sounds		◒		◒	●	
c sing a variety of songs as a member of a group	◒		○	○	◒	◒
d accompany songs using tuned and untuned instruments	●	◒	◒	●	○	◒
Level 3						
a combine sounds in order to express mood and atmosphere		●	●		○	
b invent and interpret symbols which represent particular sounds or patterns of sound	◒	◒		◒	●	
c sing a variety of songs demonstrating some control of the voice	○			○	○	◒
d play a tuned or untuned instrument as a member of a group	◒	◒	○	○	◒	◒
Level 4						
a create short musical pieces which express mood and atmosphere		◒	●			●
b interpret patterns of sounds from graphic and traditional notation	●	◒		◒	●	
c sing a variety of songs in unison and in parts, with control of phrasing, diction and tone quality	○		○	○	○	◒
d perform individually on an instrument from memory or from notation	◒	○	○	◒	●	○

Attainment Target 2: responding to music with understanding

A's So

	Unit 1	Unit 2	Unit 3	Unit 4	Unit 5	Unit 6
Level 2						
a listen attentively to live and recorded music and express their thoughts about it	◒	○	◒	◒	◒	●
b respond to familiar sounds within and beyond the classroom		○		○		◒
c imitate simple rhythmic patterns	●		◒			
Level 3						
a discuss sound pictures and patterns composed by themselves and others		●	●	○	◒	●
b listen attentively to live and recorded music and comment on simple characteristics	◒	○	◒	○	○	●
c answer simple rhythmic patterns	○					
d convey through performance, the style and mood of the music		◒	●	○		
Level 4						
a give reasons for their opinions about music they hear			○	○	◒	●
b listen attentively to music and recognise simple structures and expressive elements	○	○	◒	◒	●	●
c imitate and answer simple melodic patterns						
d make appropriate suggestions about how music should be performed		○	◒	○		

Key

○ visited

◒ explored

● main focus

What to look for on the Activity pages

Unit 5: High and low sounds

Unit 5: High and low sounds

Main Purpose
to understand that symbols can communicate levels of pitch

Main Skill
listening and recognising changes in levels of pitch and creating symbols to communicate levels of pitch

Musical Element
Main: Pitch
Other: Texture, Timbre, Dynamics, Structure

Main Stimuli
Songs: 'The old brass wagon'
'Hill an gully rida'

Main Activities
- musical games
- singing
- exploring sounds
- creating and reading from symbols
- responding to recorded music

Activity 1

Purpose: to hear the difference between high and low sounds

Resources: chime bars/metallophone, notes: C (high) and C (low)

Time guide: 5–10 minutes

Responding to high and low sounds

Play the two notes on chime bars/xylophone/metallophone. Ask the children to point to the ceiling when they hear the high sound and point to the floor when they hear the low sound. Gradually close the gap between the two notes, by playing notes closer together, so that the difference between high and low sounds is not so wide or obvious.

space for photo

82

Activity 2

Purpose: to recognise the difference between high sounds and low sounds from symbols; to perform high sounds and low sounds from symbols

Resources: copymasters 20, 21, 22, 23, 24, two C chime bars (1 high and 1 low)

Time guide: 10–15 minutes

Playing high and lo… symbols

Display the flashcard, m…

20

Ask the children:
• How do you think this …
(One high sound followe…

Allow small groups of ch…

21 22

They should perform the… xylophone, or metalloph…

Extensi… children… They sh… on the c…

Activity 3

Purpose: to hear and recognise high, middle and low sounds, and to notate the sounds

Resources: chime bars/xylophone/metallophone, notes: C,E,G

Time guide 10–15 minutes

Support point: If you are using a xylophone/metallophone/glockenspiel, rather than the chime bars, then take all the bars which the children will not be using off the instrument.

Workin…
Draw or…

high
midd…
low

Play not… the diffe… able to i…

Ask one… another… example…

Introduces the unit.

Provides useful tips relating to musical knowledge and classroom practice.

Sub-headings break section up into manageable chunks.

Words from songs included on cassettes/compact discs.

Tells you the main aim of the activity, what you need and approximately how much time is required.

Tells you what you need, approximately how much time is required, and venue (if activity cannot take place in the classroom).

What to look for on the Section pages

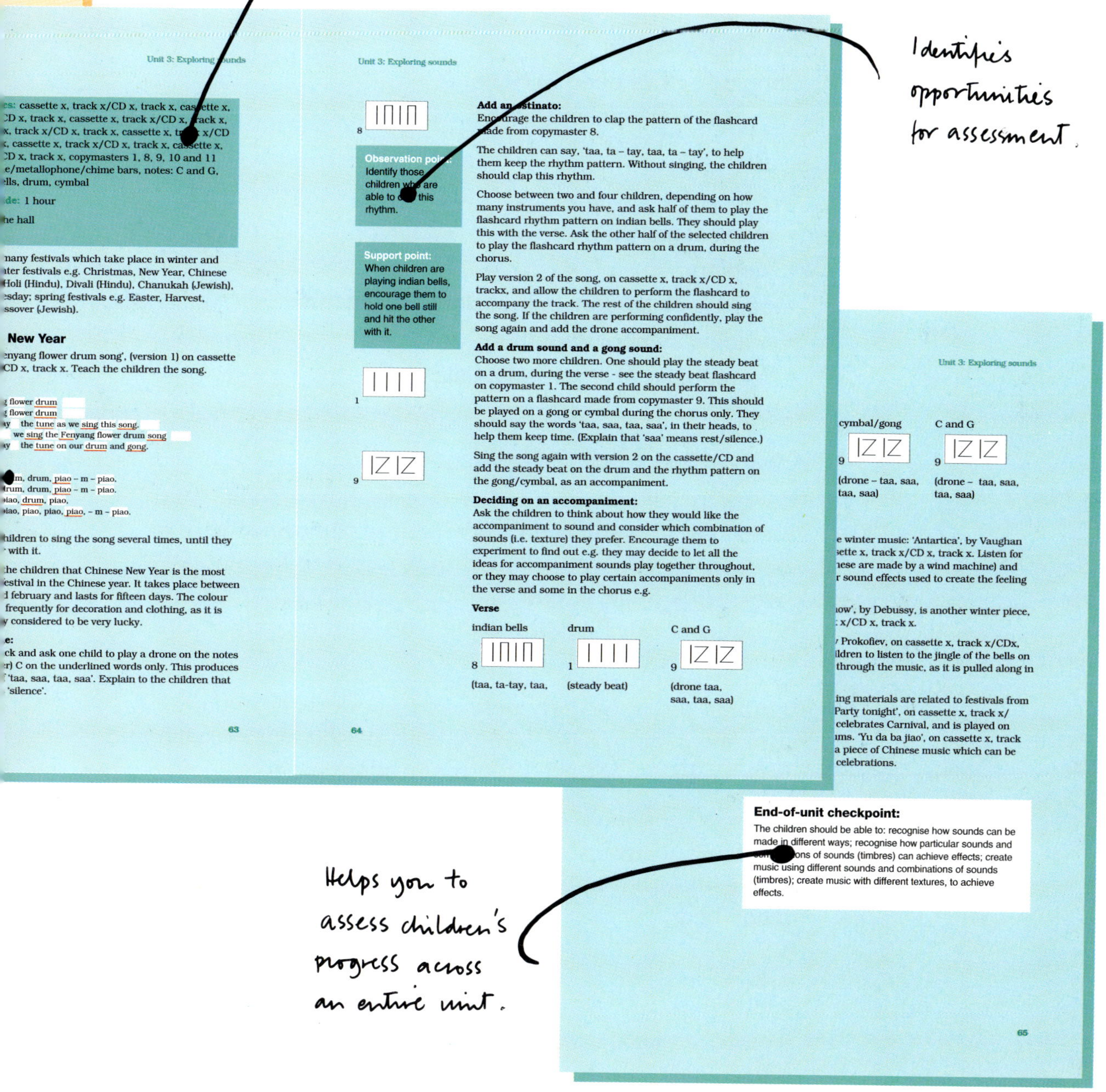

Identifies opportunities for assessment.

Helps you to assess children's progress across an entire unit.

Unit 1: Rhythm patterns

Main Purpose

to respond to rhythm patterns by listening and singing; reading from notation and playing with control; recognising and performing a steady beat

Main Skill

to sing and play simple rhythms

Musical Element

Main: Duration

Other: Texture, Structure

Main Stimuli

Songs: 'I've been to Harlem'
'A ram sam sam'
'Tideo'

Main Activities

- musical games
- singing
- playing classroom percussion instruments
- reading symbols/notation
- responding to recorded music

Activity 1

Purpose:
to develop control and accuracy when performing a steady beat

Resources:
cassette 1, track 2/CD 1, track 2

Time guide:
little and often

Keeping a steady beat

Play the track of 'King Cotton', a march by Sousa. Lead the children in keeping the steady beat of the music with a variety of body percussion sounds e.g. clap hands, pat knees, click fingers, pat shoulders. Clicks at the beginning of the musical extract will provide you with a guide to the speed of the steady beat.

Combine different body percussion sounds to make a pattern e.g. clap, clap (hands), pat, pat (knees). You should always make a pattern of four sounds.

This activity should be repeated often, to develop the children's accuracy in hearing and keeping the steady beat. Choose different children to lead the class in keeping the steady beat.

Activity 2

Purpose: to listen and respond accurately

Time guide: 10–15 minutes

Echoing rhythm patterns with beats grouped in threes and fours

Clap some rhythm patterns for the class to echo back. When you have finished clapping a rhythm, put your hands on your knees, or use another prearranged signal, to let the children know you have ended the rhythm.
The following are some examples of rhythm patterns you can use:

Rhythms in 4 beats
long, short, short, long, long
short, long, short, long, long
short, short, short, short, long, long
long, long, short, short, long

Rhythms in 3 beats
short, short, long, long
long, short, short, long
short, short, long, short, short
long, short, short, short, short

Activity 3

Purpose: to read and perform rhythm patterns from symbols

Resources: copymasters 1, 2, 3, 4, *untuned percussion instruments:* wood-block, claves, tambour, drums, finger castanets, wooden agogo

Time guide: 10–15 minutes

Support point: Write the symbols on the back of the flashcards, so that you can see the rhythm pattern. Count '1, 2, 3, 4' to get the children to begin playing together.

Performing rhythm patterns from symbols

Make flashcards from copymasters 1, 2, 3 and 4.

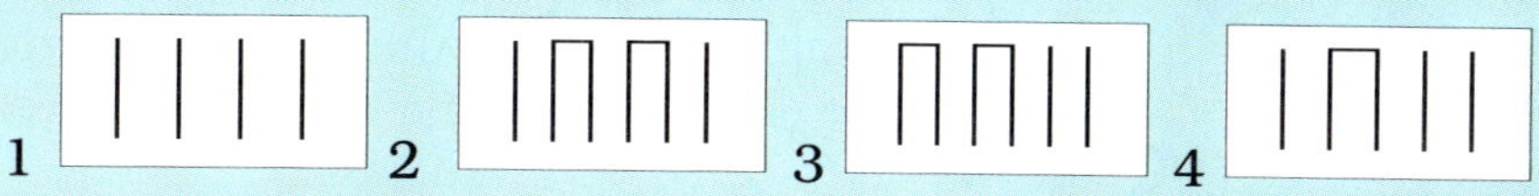

Display the first flashcard and ask the children:

- Can anyone clap this pattern?

(They should clap four equal sounds.)

Tell the children that each line on the card represents one steady beat. Count '1, 2, 3, 4', for all the children to start performing together from the flashcard.

Encourage the children to say the words on the flashcards as they clap the rhythm pattern e.g. for flashcard 1, 'taa, taa, taa, taa'. Do the same with the other flashcards. Speaking the words will help the children to clap the rhythm pattern accurately.

Extension: Allow the children to perform from the same flashcards, using percussion instruments. If you don't have enough instruments for every child in the class, divide the children into pairs and give each pair an instrument to share. The pair should take turns and the child without the instrument can perform the rhythm pattern using body percussion sounds which they have chosen.

Activity 4

Purpose:
to begin working with symbols and beats grouped in threes

Resources:
copymasters 5, 6 and 7
cassette 1, track 3/CD 1, track 3,

Time guide:
10–15 minutes

5

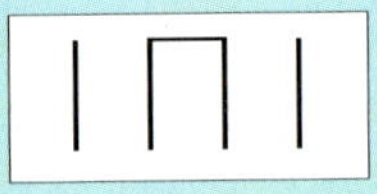
6

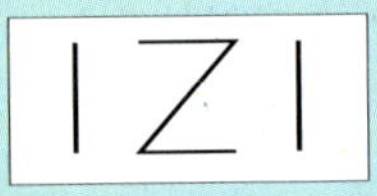
7

Working with beats grouped in threes

Make flashcards from copymasters 5,6 and 7.

Play cassette 1, track 3/CD 1, track 3. You will hear an extract from Shostakovitch's 5th symphony (2nd movement). The extract emphasises 3-beat patterns. Encourage the children to clap the first flashcard as they listen to the music. This flashcard represents a steady beat. Ask the children to keep the beat in the following way:
Beat 1 (pat knees) Beat 2 (clap hands) Beat 3 (clap hands)

Display the second flashcard and encourage the children to clap or play the new pattern to the music. They should say the words, 'taa, ta-tay, taa', as they do so.

Display the third flashcard and clap it for the children.
Ask the children:
- Which symbol is used for silence?
(the middle symbol)

Tell the children this is called a 'rest', which is referred to on the copymaster as 'saa'. Encourage the children to make a shrug with their hands to demonstrate the rest. Clap or play this pattern with the extract of music.

Activity 5

Purpose:
to begin working with rhythm patterns grouped in twos

Resources:
cassette 1, track 4/CD 1, track 4, cassette 1, track 5/CD 1, track 5

Time guide:
10–15 minutes

Rhythm patterns with beats grouped in twos

Play the first extract 'The Dance of Nymphs and Satyrs', from 'L'ile Enchanté', by Sullivan. The children should feel the way the beats are grouped in the music, by clapping on the first beat and clicking their fingers on the second beat. You will hear clicks before the music begins. These will give you the speed of the beat.

Play cassette 1, track 5/CD 1, track 5 and allow the children to become familiar with the chant 'Mosquito'. In this extract, the beats are also grouped in twos.

As the children listen to the chant, allow them to feel the two beats in each phrase by clapping on the first beat (words indicated by shading) and clicking fingers on the second beat (indicated by words underlined). Children who cannot click their fingers should flick them.

When the children are familiar with the chant, try performing it: on lines 1, 3, 5, 7 and 9, pat knees on the first beat and play the second beat by holding up the same number of fingers as the number in the rhyme; on lines 2, 4, 6, 8 and 10, play the two beats in the following way: pat knees on the first beat and clap hands on the second beat.

A mosquito one, a mosquito two,
A mosquito jump in the old man shoe.

A mosquito three, a mosquito four,
A mosquito open the old man door.

A mosquito five, a mosquito six,
A mosquito pick up the old man sticks.

A mosquito seven, a mosquito eight,
A mosquito open the old man gate.

A mosquito nine, a mosquito ten,
A mosquito biting the man a-gain.

Activity 6

Purpose:
to begin working with rhythm patterns with beats grouped in fours

Resources:
copymaster 1, cassette 1, track 6/ CD 1, track 6, cassette 1, track 7/CD 1, track 7

Time guide:
10–15 minutes

Rhythm patterns with beats grouped in fours

Display the flashcard on copymaster 1.
Ask the children:
- How many steady beats are on the card?
(four steady beats)

Say '1, 2, 3, 4', for the children to begin playing together and ask them to perform the flashcard in the following way:

beat 1	beat 2	beat 3	beat 4
(clap hands)	(punch hand)	(punch hand)	(punch hand)

Performing the flashcard this way emphasises the first beat each time and shows that the beats are grouped in fours.

Play 'Shine' by Dabney, Mack and Brown. Using the body percussion sequence, clap hands, punch hand, punch hand, punch hand, keep the steady beat of the music.

Play the second extract, on cassette 1, track 7/CD 1, track 7, and teach the children 'When the saints go marching in'. This song also has groups of four beats together.

1

Oh when the saints, ____ ____ Go marching in ____ ____, oh when the
saints go march-ing in ____ ____ I wanna
be ____ in that number ____ ____. When the
saints go march-ing in.

The first beat is shown by shading. The second, third and fourth beats are indicated by lines and underlined words. When the children are familiar with the song, they can add the body percussion sequence: clap, punch hand, punch hand, punch hand. Children who are confident with this activity can play the group of four beats on percussion instruments e.g. play the drum on beat 1 and let wood-blocks and tambours play a single sound on beats 2, 3 and 4.

Section 1

Resources: cassette 1, track 8/CD 1, track 8, cassette 1, track 9/CD 1, track 9, cassette 1, track 10/CD 1, track 10, cassette 1, track 11/CD 1, track 11, cassette 1, track 12/CD 1, track 12, *untuned percussion instruments:* wooden agogo, wood-block, tambour, drums, metal agogo, cow-bell, triangle etc.

Time guide: 1 hour

Singing and keeping the steady beat with percussion instruments

Play the track 'I've been to Harlem' (version 1) on cassette 1, track 8/CD 1, track 8, and clap the steady beat of the music while you listen. The steady beat is indicated by the shaded words.

I've been to Har-lem. I've been to Do-ver,
I've travelled this wide world all o-ver,
O-ver, o-ver, three times o-ver,
Drink what you want to drink and turn the glasses o-ver.
Sail-ing east, sail-ing west, sail-ing o-ver the o - cean,
Better watch out when the boat beg-ins to rock,
Or you'll lose your girl in the o - cean.

Repeat this activity and ask the children to listen to the beats in the music and think about how they are grouped. Encourage the children to identify that the beats are grouped in fours.

Play the track again and, this time, encourage the children to sing the song. When the children are confident with singing the song with the cassette/CD, sing it again and, this time, allow four to six children to play the steady beat on the tambour/wood-block/wooden agogo/claves.

Play a rhythm round

Play cassette 1, track 9/CD 1, track 9 (version 1), 'A ram sam sam'. Lead the children in saying the words rhythmically. The steady beat is indicated by the shaded words.

A ram sam sam, a ram sam sam, (8)
Guli guli guli guli guli ram sam sam. (13)
A-rav-i, a-rav-i. (6)
Guli guli guli guli guli ram sam sam. (13)

Support point: Encourage the children to say the words aloud or in their heads as they clap the rhythm.

Demonstrate the rhythm to the children by clapping each line separately. Ask them to clap the rhythm back to you. They should clap once on each syllable and keep to the speed and emphasis of the words as they would be spoken.

Observation point: Identify those children who are confidently clapping the rhythm of each line.

If the children are not clapping the rhythm carefully enough, clap one line at a time and ask them to count how many claps you made. (The answers are indicated above.)

Practise clapping the rhythm in different ways:

1 You clap the first line, the children clap the second line and so on.

2 The children clap the first line, you clap the second line and so on.

3 Divide the class into two halves. The first half clap the first line and so on.

Support point: If you have a small class, don't divide the children into two groups to play the round. You can use the cassette/CD to play the first part of the round. The class can perform the second part.

When the children are familiar with clapping the rhythm of this rhyme, encourage them to try to perform the rhyme as a rhythm 'round':

Divide the class into two groups. The first group should clap the rhythm. The second group should tap the rhythm. The second group should begin when the first half reaches the third line, so that both groups will clap the word 'A' together.

Performing a round using percussion

Encourage the children to choose untuned percussion instruments. They should choose instruments which will be suitable for playing a rhythm. Ask the children:

- Which instruments are better for playing rhythms?

(A shaking instrument is unsuitable, unless tapped, because it will not play a precise beat. An instrument which can be tapped is appropriate for this reason.)

Sort the instruments into groups, according to the timbre of their sounds i.e. wooden instruments, metal instruments, shaking and scraping instruments.

Select sixteen children and divide them into four groups of four children. Each group should have instruments of the same timbre. These children should play the rhythm pattern of 'A ram sam sam' on instruments, while the rest of the children clap/tap knees to the rhythm.

Listening

Play the following extracts:

1 'Lincolnshire poacher' arranged by D. Broadbent (Beats grouped in twos) on cassette 1, track 10/CD 1, track 10

2 'Blue Danube waltz', by Johann Strauss (Beats grouped in threes) on cassette cassette 1, track 11/CD 1, track 11

3 'Silence is golden', by 'Gaudio and Crewe' (Beats grouped in fours) on cassette 1, track 12/CD 1, track 12

Ask the children:
- How are the beats grouped together?

To help the children find the answer, you can experiment in the following way:

1 If the music has a 2-beat rhythm pattern then the children will be able to perform the following rhythm pattern: clap hands, click/flick fingers.

2 If the music has a 3-beat rhythm pattern then the children will be able to perform the following rhythm pattern to accompany the music: tap knees, clap hands, clap hands.

3 If the music has a 4-beat rhythm pattern then the children will be able to perform the following rhythm pattern: clap hands, punch hand, punch hand, punch hand.

Extension: Allow the children to work in pairs. Each child should choose an instrument, making sure it has a different timbre to that of their partner. Together the two children can perform 'A ram sam sam', with which they are already familiar, as a rhythm round.

Encourage the children to tape record their peformances.

Section 2

Resources: cassette 1, track 8/CD 1, track 8, cassette 1, track 13/CD 1, track 13, cassette 1, track 14/CD 1, track 14, cassette 1, track 15/CD 1, track 15, cassette 1, track 16/CD 1, track 16, copymaster 4, *untuned percussion instruments:* tambour, wood-block, wooden agogo, finger castanets

Time guide: 1 hour

Where: the hall

Accompanying a song with rhythm patterns and performing from symbols

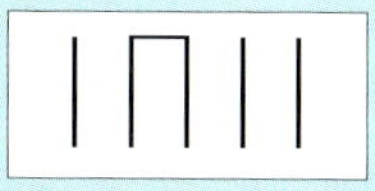

4

Play cassette 1, track 8/CD 1, track 8 and sing the song, 'I've been to Harlem' (version 1). The children should already be familiar with this song from their work in Section 1.

Display the flashcard on copymaster 4.

Ask the children:

- Can anyone clap this?

(The pattern they should clap is long, short, short, long, long. Encourage the children to say the words, 'taa, ta-tay, taa, taa'.)

Encourage all the children to practise clapping the pattern and saying 'taa, taa-tay, taa, taa'. Use either of the following two prearranged signals to start the children clapping together: count '1, 2, 3, 4', or say 'and'.

Play the track again. Ask the children to listen to the song. Ask them:

- Which words in the song fit the rhythm pattern on the flashcard?

('I've been to Harlem', 'I've been to Dover', 'I've travelled this wide'.)

Take one of the children's suggestions, e.g. 'I've been to Harlem', and encourage the children to look at the card and clap the rhythm pattern on it, saying the words 'I've been to Harlem' as they do so. Count '1, 2, 3, 4', or say 'and', to start the children performing together.

Observation point: Try to identify those children who find it easy to clap the rhythm whilst the other half of the class is singing.

Divide the class in half. Let the first half clap the rhythm on the flashcard. Ask the second half to sing the song on cassette 1, track 13/CD 1, track 13, (version 2). On this version of the song, the steady beat and the rhythm pattern can be heard.

The first half of the class should keep saying the words 'I've been to Harlem', as they clap, otherwise they will start clapping what the singers are singing.

Swop the two groups around so that the singers clap the rhythm and the clappers get a chance to sing.

Accompanying a song with percussion

Observation point: Try to identify those children who choose instruments which are appropriate for playing rhythm (instruments which can be tapped).

Choose three or four of those children who you were able to identify in the previous activity as being confident to clap the rhythm throughout the singing.

Ask those children to choose untuned percussion instruments on which to play the same rhythm. The rest of the class should sing the song with cassette 1, track 13/ CD 1, track 13, version 2.

Remind the children playing instruments to keep saying the words, 'I've been to Harlem', to themselves.

Listening

Play cassette 1, track 14/CD 1, track 14 and ask the children to listen to an extract called 'Kwacheri', a traditional song from Kenya, which has a rhythm pattern that is played throughout the song. The pattern is played by drums and claves.

The second extract, on cassette 1, track 15/ CD 1, track 15, is a recorder piece called 'Dont vient cela' by Susato. This also has a rhythm pattern which is played throughout. Ask the children to listen to these rhythm patterns.

Explain to the children that when a rhythm pattern is repeated continuously in this way, it is called an ostinato. Encourage the children to identify that the rhythm pattern for 'I've been to Harlem', which the children have been playing, is also an ostinato.

Singing 'A ram sam sam' in a round

Play cassette 1, track 16/CD 1, track 16, 'A ram sam sam', version 2.

The children should already be familiar with the words to 'A ram sam sam'. You can now teach them the tune to the song. 'A ram sam sam' is a song from Morocco.

When the children are familiar with the tune, they can sing the song as a round with the cassette/CD. The children should start singing when the tape reaches the beginning of the third line - both groups should sing the first word together.

The children will find it easier to sing this as a round as they have already performed the rhythm of the words in a round.

Singing and dancing in a round

Teach the children the 'A ram sam sam' dance. Ask them to stand in a circle.

1 A ram sam sam, a ram sam sam,
2 Guli guli guli guli guli ram sam sam.
3 A rav-i , a rav-i
4 Guli guli guli guli guli ram sam sam.

Support point: Encourage the children to listen very carefully, so that they keep with the beat and don't dance too quickly.

Line 1: Starting with your right foot, take two steps forwards and then two steps back. Step on the steady beat (as indicated by the shaded words).

Line 2: Keeping on the spot, turn in a circle towards your right. After you turn, stamp your feet (right, left, right) in time to the words 'ram sam sam'.

Line 3: Everybody in the circle hold hands and raise arms upwards on 'ra' and lower them on 'vi' of 'ravi'. Bend your knees as you raise your arms and straighten your knees as you lower your arms. Repeat this movement.

LIne 4: Drop hands then turn in a circle on the spot, towards your left. After you turn, stamp your feet (left, right, left) in time to the words 'ram sam sam'.

Practise performing the dance with the track, without singing. When the children are performing the dance confidently, let them sing at the same time. Sing the song as a round and perform the dance as a round by dividing the class into two groups.

Section 3

Resources: cassette 1, track 13/CD 1, track 13, cassette 1, track 17/CD 1, track 17, cassette 1, track 14/CD 1, track 14, cassette 1, track 15/CD 1, track 15, cassette 1, track 18/CD 1, track 18, cassette 1, track 19/CD 1, track 19, cassette 1, track 20/CD 1, track 20, copymasters 3 and 4, *untuned percussion instruments:* tambour, wood-block, wooden agogo, drum

Time guide: 1 hour

Accompanying 'I've been to Harlem' with rhythm patterns and performing from flashcards

Play cassette 1, track 13/CD 1, track 13 (version 2) 'I've been to Harlem', and sing the song. Display the flashcard used in Section 2 (Copymaster 4).

4

Ask the children:
- Can anyone remember which words this fits in the song?

('I've been to Harlem')

Ask for a volunteer to clap/play the flashcard for you. Encourage the child to say 'Taa, ta-tay, taa, taa' as he/she plays/claps. Display a new flashcard made from copymaster 3.

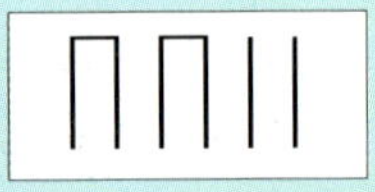
3

Ask the children:
- Can anyone clap this?

(ta-tay, ta-tay, taa, taa)

Ask the children:
- Can anyone tell me which words fit this pattern?

Allow the children to listen to the song again, very carefully. Encourage the children to identify that the rhythm pattern falls on the words, 'Turn the glasses over' (line 4) and 'boat begins to rock or' (line 6).

Play cassette 1, track 17/CD 1, track 17 (version 3). This demonstrates the steady beat and two rhythm patterns. Encourage the class to clap the pattern 'Ta-tay, ta-tay, taa, taa' to the music, without singing. Remind them to keep saying the word pattern e.g. 'Turn the glasses over' in their heads as they clap.

Observation Point: Identify those children who are able to recognise the rhythm patterns.

Display the two flashcards. Count '1, 2, 3, 4', for the children to start clapping together and alternate between the two flashcards. Encourage the children to clap the patterns shown, without the cassette/CD.

Support Point:
If you prefer, say, 'Taa, ta-tay, taa, taa' ,for 'I've been to Harlem', and 'Ta-tay, ta-tay, taa, taa', instead of, 'Turn the glasses over'.

I've been to Harlem

turn the glasses over

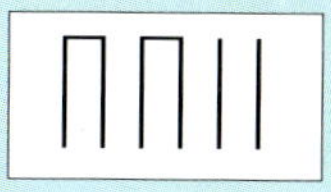

I've been to Harlem

turn the glasses over

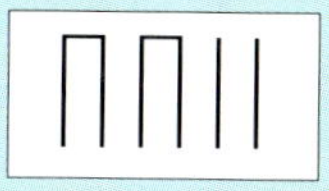

Choose four to six children and ask them to choose untuned percussion instruments, and let half of them perform from the first flashcard, and the other two or three perform the second flashcard. Encourage these children to perform the rhythms repeatedly (ostinato), reading from the flashcards whilst the rest of the class sing the song with cassette 1, track 17/CD 1, track 17, version 3.

Listening

Play 'kwacheri' again on cassette 1, track 14/CD 1, track 14, and 'Dont vient' on cassette 1, track 15/CD 1, track 15. These extracts should already be familiar from Section 2. Encourage the children to clap the rhythm of the accompaniment for each extract, with the recording.

Singing 'Tideo'

Play cassette 1, track 18/CD 1, track 18, version 1. Teach the children the American folk song, 'Tideo'. The steady beat is indicated by the shading.

Pass one window, ti-de-o,
Pass two windows, ti-de-o,
Pass three windows, ti-de-o,
Jingle at the windows, ti-de-o.

Refrain: Ti-de-o, ti-de-o,
Clap at the windows, ti-de-o.

When the children are familiar with the song, display the two flashcards made from copymasters 3 and 4.

Ask the children:

- Do any of the words in this song fit the rhythm patterns for the first flashcard?

The children should listen to this piece again and identify 'Clap at the window' fits this flashcard.

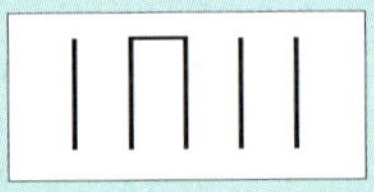

4

Hold up the second flashcard and ask the same question. Play the track again and encourage the children to identify that 'Jingle at the window' fits this flashcard.

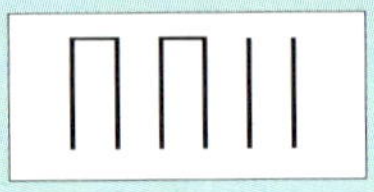

3

Extension: Display the two flashcards. The children should alternate between playing and singing first one and then the other.

4

Clap at the window

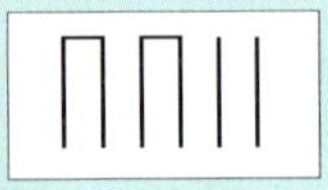

3

jingle at the window

4

clap at the window

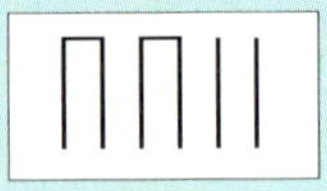

3

jingle at the window

Version 1 of the song, on cassette 1, track 18/CD 1, track 18, can be used for teaching the children the song. Version 2 of the song, on cassette 1, track 19/CD 1, track 19, has the rhythm on the first flashcard added. Version 3, on cassette 1, track 20/CD 1, track 20, has both rhythm patterns and the steady beat added to the song.

The children will find it easier to sing this as a round as they have already performed the rhythm of the words in a round.

Singing and dancing in a round

Teach the children the 'A ram sam sam' dance. Ask them to stand in a circle.

1 A ram sam sam, a ram sam sam,
2 Guli guli guli guli guli ram sam sam.
3 A rav-i , a rav-i
4 Guli guli guli guli guli ram sam sam.

Support point: Encourage the children to listen very carefully, so that they keep with the beat and don't dance too quickly.

Line 1: Starting with your right foot, take two steps forwards and then two steps back. Step on the steady beat (as indicated by the shaded words).

Line 2: Keeping on the spot, turn in a circle towards your right. After you turn, stamp your feet (right, left, right) in time to the words 'ram sam sam'.

Line 3: Everybody in the circle hold hands and raise arms upwards on 'ra' and lower them on 'vi' of 'ravi'. Bend your knees as you raise your arms and straighten your knees as you lower your arms. Repeat this movement.

LIne 4: Drop hands then turn in a circle on the spot, towards your left. After you turn, stamp your feet (left, right, left) in time to the words 'ram sam sam'.

Practise performing the dance with the track, without singing. When the children are performing the dance confidently, let them sing at the same time. Sing the song as a round and perform the dance as a round by dividing the class into two groups.

Section 3

Resources: cassette 1, track 13/CD 1, track 13, cassette 1, track 17/CD 1, track 17, cassette 1, track 14/CD 1, track 14, cassette 1, track 15/CD 1, track 15, cassette 1, track 18/CD 1, track 18, cassette 1, track 19/CD 1, track 19, cassette 1, track 20/CD 1, track 20, copymasters 3 and 4, *untuned percussion instruments:* tambour, wood-block, wooden agogo, drum

Time guide: 1 hour

Accompanying 'I've been to Harlem' with rhythm patterns and performing from flashcards

Play cassette 1, track 13/CD 1, track 13 (version 2) 'I've been to Harlem', and sing the song. Display the flashcard used in Section 2 (Copymaster 4).

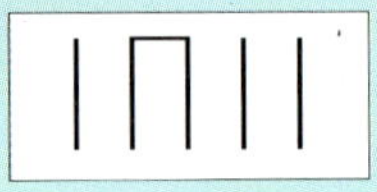
4

Ask the children:
- Can anyone remember which words this fits in the song?
('I've been to Harlem')

Ask for a volunteer to clap/play the flashcard for you. Encourage the child to say 'Taa, ta-tay, taa, taa' as he/she plays/claps. Display a new flashcard made from copymaster 3.

3

Ask the children:
- Can anyone clap this?
(ta-tay, ta-tay, taa, taa)

Ask the children:
- Can anyone tell me which words fit this pattern?

Allow the children to listen to the song again, very carefully. Encourage the children to identify that the rhythm pattern falls on the words, 'Turn the glasses over' (line 4) and 'boat begins to rock or' (line 6).

Play cassette 1, track 17/CD 1, track 17 (version 3). This demonstrates the steady beat and two rhythm patterns. Encourage the class to clap the pattern 'Ta-tay, ta-tay, taa, taa' to the music, without singing. Remind them to keep saying the word pattern e.g. 'Turn the glasses over' in their heads as they clap.

Observation Point: Identify those children who are able to recognise the rhythm patterns.

Display the two flashcards. Count '1, 2, 3, 4', for the children to start clapping together and alternate between the two flashcards. Encourage the children to clap the patterns shown, without the cassette/CD.

Section 4

Resources: cassette 1, track 22/CD 1, track 22, cassette 1, track 23/CD 1, track 23, cassette 1, track 24/CD 1, track 24, cassette 1, track 25/CD 1, track 25, cassette 1, track 26/CD 1, track 26, cassette 1, track 27/CD 1, track 27, cassette 1, track 18/CD 1, track 18, cassette 1, track 21/CD 1, track 21, copymasters 3 and 4, *tuned percussion instruments:* xylophone/metallophone/chime bars: notes, G and (lower) C

Time guide: 1 hour

Adding a drone and ostinato patterns to 'Tideo'

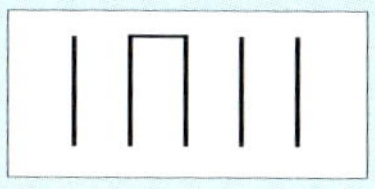

4

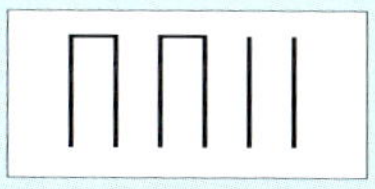

3

Play cassette 1, track 18/CD 1, track 18, version 1 of 'Tideo'. Sing the song and tap the steady beat throughout, encouraging the children to copy you.

Choose one or two children and allow them to play a drone on notes C and G on the xylophone. They should play the two notes simultaneously on the steady beat.

Support point:
C should be a lower note than G. (Remember that 'L' stands for the longest, lowest notes on the left.)

The rest of the class should sing the song with version 1.

Play 'Tideo', version 4, on cassette 1, track 21/CD 1, track 21, and display a flashcard made from copymasters 3 and 4.

Choose children to perform these rhythms on untuned percussion instruments.

On version 4 of 'Tideo', you can hear these two rhythm patterns as well as a drone.

Observation point:
Identify those children who are able to play the accompaniment patterns confidently.

Perform the song again and let other children perform the accompaniment patterns.

Extension: Add to 'I've been to Harlem', the accompaniment rhythm patterns on copymasters 3 and 4 and a drone. You should use notes F and C to play the drone with this song. These accompaniment patterns can be heard on version 4 of the song on cassette 1, track 22/CD 1, track 22.

Listening

Play cassette 1, track 23/CD 1, track 23, 'Rise up o flame'. This song has an accompaniment drone which is played on the violin. The drone can be heard underneath the singing in a round. Explain to the children that the other instrument which they are able to hear is called a psaltery.

The second extract, on cassette 1, track 24/CD 1, track 24, is. 'Cantiga: como per sas culpas os omes', by Alphonso the

Wise (1221) played on the hurdy gurdy. The hurdy gurdy, a string instrument, plays the drone and the tune simultaneously.

Dancing to 'Tideo'

Play 'Tideo', version 1, on cassette 1, track 18/CD 1, track 18.

You can do the following dance to this song:

1 All the children should stand in a circle with their arms forming arches.

2 One child should travel in and out of the arches.

3 On the first line of the refrain, they should stop in front of the person they have reached or are closest to. They should proceed to make the following actions on 'tideo':
  i Tap knees on 'ti'.
  ii Clap hands on 'de'.
  iii Clap hands on those of person facing, on 'o'.
  They should repeat this series of actions on the second 'tideo'. The rest of the class should tap their knees and clap their own hands twice, in time with these actions.

4 For the second line of the refrain 'Clap at the windows ti-de-o', everybody should clap once on each of the four steady beats in the line.

When children have had more practice with this activity, the child moving in and out of the arches can prearrange which body percussion actions he/she will use at the beginning of the refrain e.g. clap hands four times, stamp feet four times, click fingers four times. The child should also alter the words of the last line, to accommodate their change e.g. 'clap/stamp/click at the windows, ti-de-o'.

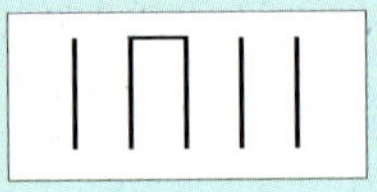
4

Extension: For the following activity, you will need to use the flashcard on copymaster 4.

The following song is called 'Land of the silver birch'. Teach the children the song using version 1 of the song on cassette 1, track 25/CD 1, track 25.

1 Land of the silver birch, home of the bea-ver,
Where still the mighty moose wanders at will,
Blue lake and rocky shore, I will return once more.
Hi hiya hiya, hi hiya hiya, hi hiya hiya, hi ya.

2 Down in the for-est, deep in the low lands,
My heart cries out for you, hills of the north.
Blue lake and rocky shore, I will return once more.
Hi hiya hiya, hi hiya hiya, hi hiya hiya, hi ya.

Support point: Make sure that the children use F rather than F#.

Ask the children:

- Which words fit the flashcard's rhythm?

('Home of the beaver', and, 'Deep in the lowlands'.)

This rhythm can be heard on version 2 of the song on cassette 1, track 26/CD 1, track 26.

The drone notes for this song are D and A on your tuned percussion instrument. The drone can be heard on version 3 of the song on cassette 1, track 27/CD 1, track 27.

With the exception of the song 'A ram sam sam', all of the songs in Unit 1 are based on a pentatonic (five note) scale. ('I've been to Harlem' uses notes: F, G, A, C, D; 'Tideo' uses notes: C, D, E, G, A; 'Land of the silver birch' uses notes: F, G, A, C, D.)

Extension: Let the children create their own rhythm patterns on tuned percussion instruments, to accompany the songs: version 4 of 'I've been to Harlem', cassette 1, track 22/CD 1, track 22 and 'Tideo' (version 4), cassette 1, track 21/CD 1, track 21 and version 3 of 'Land of the silver birch', cassette 1, track 27/CD 1, track 27.

They should play the rhythm on one of the flashcards e.g. copymaster 3. They should use the notes which fit their song (see above).

End-of-unit checkpoint:

Children should be able to show their understanding of rhythm patterns by performing rhythm patterns using long and short sounds; performing from notation (flashcards) to accompany songs; listening and responding to music through discussion; composing their own accompaniments.

Unit 2: Higher and lower sounds getting into shape

Main Purpose

to recognise the difference between pitched sounds made on tuned instruments and unpitched sounds made on untuned instruments; to use these sounds to create a musical shape

Main Skill

listening to, recognising and performing pitched/unpitched sounds on tuned/untuned instruments; creating a musical shape (ABA structure)

Musical Element

Main: Pitch, Structure

Other: Duration, Dynamics, Tempo

Main Stimuli

Song - 'Doctor Foster'

Poem - 'Listen to the sound'

Main Activities

- musical games
- exploring sounds
- creating effects
- singing
- responding to recorded music

Activity 1

Purpose:
to explore the sounds made by different percussion instruments

Resources:
Group 1: *two-tone percussion instruments and tuned instruments* e.g. wooden agogo, metal agogo, two-tone wood-block, bongo drums, xylophone, metallophone,

Exploring game

Ask the children to sit in a circle. Place the instruments in the middle of the circle. Encourage the children to explore the instruments. Ask them:

- Which instruments can make both high and low sounds? (wooden agogo, metal agogo, two-tone wood-block, bongo drums, xylophone, metallophone, glockenspiel)

- Which instruments make one sound, either high or low? (cymbal, tambour, cabasa, claves, pop jingle, guiro)

If you do not have these instruments, you should ask the children to categorise those instruments you do have into either Group 1 (two-tone and tuned percussion instruments)

glockenspiel; **Group 2:** *one-tone percussion instruments* e.g. cymbal, tambour, cabasa, claves, pop jingle, guiro

Time guide:
20–25 minutes

or Group 2 (one-tone percussion instruments).

The following are ways in which you can play two-tone and tuned percussion to produce both high and low sounds:

High sounds

wooden/metal agogo - tap the smaller of the two tubes; xylophone/metallophone/glockenspiel – play the smallest bars; bongo drums – play the smaller drum

Low sounds

wooden/metal agogo – tap the larger of the two tubes; xylophone/metallophone/glockenspiel – play the longer bars; bongo drums – play the larger drum

Support point:
With certain instruments, you will need to listen very carefully to find and identify the highest and lowest sounds e.g. gato drum.

Activity 2

Purpose:
to allow children to freely explore sounds made by percussion instruments

Resources:
a range of percussion instruments

Time guide:
10–15 minutes

Making two different sounds on a percussion instrument

Ask the children to sit in a circle. Give each child a percussion instrument and instruct them to place it on the floor in front of them. (Whichever instruments you have in school can be used for this activity.) Use a prearranged signal to instruct the children to pick their instruments up.

Allow each child to make one sound only on their instrument until each child has had a turn.

Ask the children to make two different sounds on their instrument. Encourage the children to think carefully and creatively about what types of sounds they would like to make e.g. tap the guiro, instead of scraping it.

Activity 3

Purpose:
to develop awareness of high and low sounds and perform from symbols

Resources:
large paper/board and marker pens, xylophone. metallophone, glockenspiel

Time guide:
5 minutes

Performing high and low pitched sounds from symbols

Draw flowing contour lines randomly on the board or on your paper e.g.

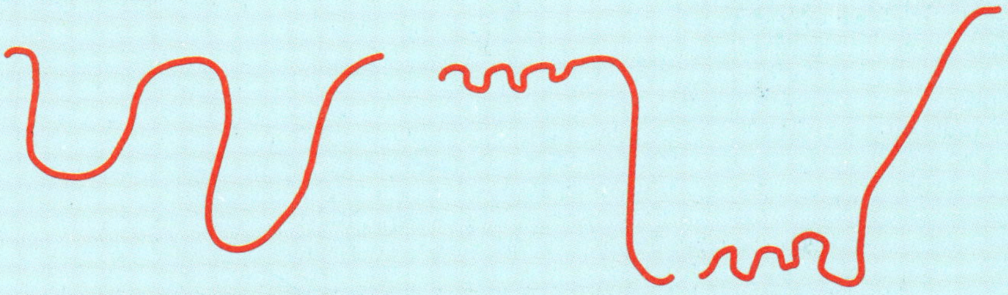

Trace your finger along the curves of the contour. As your finger moves upwards, encourage the children to make their voices go up also. As your finger moves downwards, encourage the children to make their voices do likewise.

Extension: If you have a xylophone, metallophone, or glockenspiel, encourage pairs of children to play the high notes and low notes as your finger follows the contours of your drawing.

Encourage children to compose their own contour line. They should then play the line on an instrument or using their voice.

Activity 4

Purpose:
to develop awareness and skills in creating a simple 3 part musical structure

Resources:
pitch contours created in Activity 3

Time guide:
15–20 minutes

Performing a simple musical structure using pitched and unpitched sounds

Encourage the children to suggest simple sequences of body percussion sounds e.g. rub hands, stamp foot, pat knees. These sounds are not pitched and will later become the unpitched section of the structure.

Ask the children to create symbols to represent the body percussion sounds which they have suggested e.g.

rub hands 

stamp foot 

pat knees 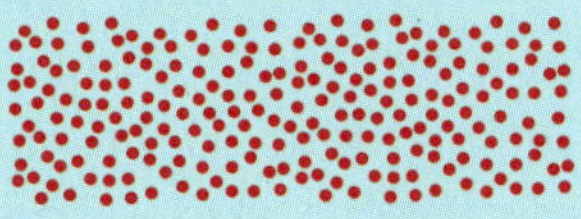

The children should practise performing from these symbols. Next, encourage the children to develop a simple sound piece from a contoured line (as in Activity 3).

The children should play the following sequence of sounds.

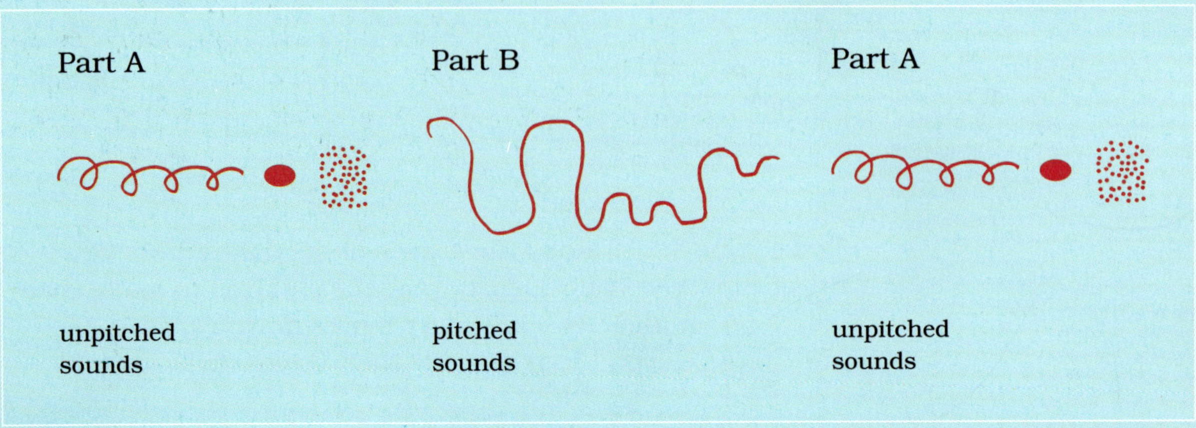

Extension: This ABA musical structure can be played on percussion instruments. Divide the children into small groups (Part A and Part B). The children could use the following sounds as an alternative to their body percussion:

Part A: unpitched sounds – untuned percussion instruments e.g. wood-block, guiro, tambour

Part B: pitched sounds – tuned percussion instruments e.g. xylophone, metallophone, chime bars

Part A: unpitched sounds - untuned percussion instruments e.g. wood-block, guiro, tambour

Activity 5

Purpose: to build a repertoire of the sounds from different instrument groups

Resources: *a range of percussion instruments:* wooden agogo, metal agogo, two-tone wood-block, bongo drums, xylophone, metallophone, cymbal, tambour, cabasa, claves, 5 large pieces of card labelled 'wood', 'metal', 'skin', 'shake', 'scrape'

Sorting percussion instruments into timbre groups

Ask the children to sit in a circle. Place the instruments and the labelled cards in the middle of the circle. Allow individual children to select an instrument, make a sound on it and then decide which label to place it next to. Ask the children:

- What material is the part of the instrument that makes the sound?
- How do you play the instrument?

Certain instruments may be more difficult to identify because they are made of more than one material, or can be played in more than one way. If you are unable to classify an instrument at all, do not be concerned as the main point of the activity is to explore and discuss types of sounds.

Cross-curricular links: **Art**

Draw, paint, use pastels and try printing from and painting string to make patterns of contoured lines.

Cross-curricular links: **Science**

Create echo sounds by beating boxes. Investigate how the volume of the box affects the sound produced. Find areas of the school where vocal echo sounds can be made e.g. gym, empty classroom. Investigate the differences between areas where the sound can be produced and where it cannot.

Section 1

Resources: cassette 2, track 2/CD 1, track 28, cassette 2, track 3/CD 1, track 29, chime bars/xylophone/glockenspiel: notes, F and C, drums, wood-blocks, cymbals, indian bells, triangles, maracas, cabasa

Time guide: 1 hour

Singing 'Doctor Foster'

Play cassette 2, track 2/CD 1, track 28. Teach the children 'Doctor Foster'.

Doctor Foster went to Glo'ster
In a show'r of rain,
He stepp'd in a puddle
Right up to his middle,
And never went there a - gain!

Sing the song again and tap the steady beat (as indicated) using two fingers to tap the palm of the other hand. Clap the rhythm of the words 'Doctor Foster went to Glo'ster', and encourage the class to copy you. Play the track again and, without singing, accompany the tape by tapping this rhythm repeatedly.

Divide the class into two groups. Let one half tap the steady beat using two fingers, and the other half use cupped hands to perform the rhythm of the first line with the track. As before, they should do this without singing.

Encourage two or three children to choose untuned percussion instruments that would make appropriate sounds to represent rain. Let them play the rhythm pattern of the first line with the track. The rest of the class should tap the steady beat and sing the song with the track.

The children playing the instruments will need to keep saying the words of the first line, to help them keep to the rhythm pattern. Repeat the song again and let different children play the rhythm of the words.

Identify those children who coped well with playing the rhythm while the rest of the class sang. Choose one of them to play the same rhythm pattern on the following notes.

F	F	C'	C'	F	F	C	C
Doc-	tor	Fo-	ster	went	to	Glo'ster	

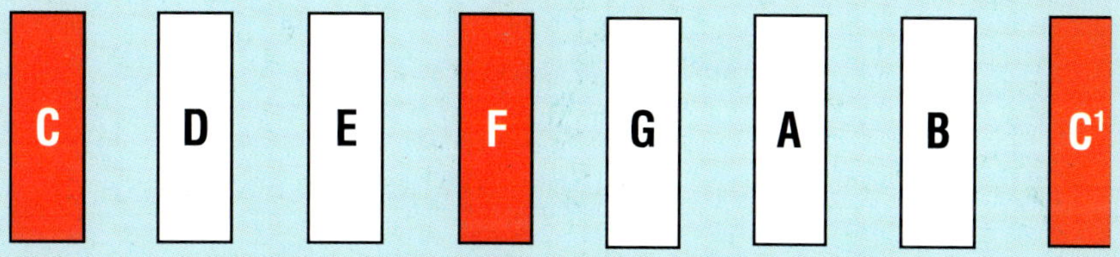

This can be repeated throughout the song.

Choose a group of children to play the rhythm pattern of the words on untuned percussion instruments, as before. The rest of the class can play the steady beat by tapping. Sing the song with the track. The children should add these sound patterns in accompaniment.

Creating 'rain' and 'puddle' sounds using body percussion and untuned percussion instruments

Observation point: Identify those children who are able to recognise and identify untuned percussion instruments, choose appropriate instruments, or body percussion, for their sound piece and think about whether the sounds should be loud/quiet.

Talk about the sounds that rain makes - gentle sounds, pitter patter sounds, splashing/dripping sounds.

Ask the children:

- Should the sounds be loud/quiet?
- Should the sounds be fast/slow?
- Should the sounds have a rhythm pattern or be played randomly?
- What type of sounds would you use? Encourage them to suggest an instrument group e.g. wooden/shaking.
- What happens when you throw a stone into a puddle?

Ripples should form on the surface of the water. Encourage the children to suggest ways in which they could make ripples of sound e.g. long sounds played on the cymbal/triangle/indian bells.

Support point: It is important to record sounds, as it is difficult for children to perform and listen and appraise simultaneously.

Divide the children into groups of four to six children. Ask them to explore and create the sound of rain or puddles, using body percussion and untuned percussion instruments.

Allow the children time to explore their sounds and use a prearranged signal e.g. put your hand in the air, to ensure that they all stop playing together. Share and record what each group has found.

(Encourage the children to write down in words which instruments they played, or body percussion they used, in sequence, so that they can play their sound piece again.)

Listening

Play 'Kalinka' on cassette 2, track 3/CD 1, track 29. This is a traditional Russian song. Ask the children:

- Is the music all the same?

Encourage them to suggest that the music is different in the middle section.

- How many sections did you hear?

(three sections)

- Are any of the sections the same?

(the first and last section)

Explain to the children that this is called an ABA structure: the first section is A, then there is a new section – B, and the last section is the same as the first – A.

This pattern can also be represented by a drawn pattern.

Extension: Encourage the children to draw/paint their own ABA pattern. Play them cassette 2, track 3/CD 1, track 29 again, and ask the children to draw designs which they feel reflect the mood of the music.

Cross-curricular links: Science and Technology

Make instruments to measure weather phenomena e.g. rain gauge, wind meter. Write weather reports and try predicting the weather for the following day/week.

Section 2

Resources: cassette 2, track 3/CD 1, track 29, cassette 2, track 2/CD 1, track 28, cassette 2, track 4/CD 1, track 30, a range of tuned and untuned percussion instruments, a tape recorder

Time guide: 1 hour

Listening

Play cassette 2, track 3/CD 1, track 29, 'Kalinka' . The children will already be familiar with this piece, from Section 1. Ask the children:

- Can you remember how many sections this music has? (three sections – ABA structure)

Encourage the children to show recognition of the different sections by responding with different actions e.g. Section A – clap hands; Section B – make circular movements with hands in the air; Section A – clap hands again.

Creating a sound piece

Explain to the children that they are going to create an ABA structured sound piece, in the following way: They will sing 'Doctor Foster' with an accompaniment– this will be part A. Next, they will choose a sound piece from those they composed in Section 1 – this will be part B. Finally, they will sing the song with accompaniment again – part A.

The class should decide, through discussion, which sound piece to use for part B, a 'rain' sound piece, or a 'puddle' sound piece. (Ensure that the children remember which instruments, and in what sequence, they should play.)

Next, play 'Doctor Foster', on cassette 2, track 2/CD 1, track 28, and practise singing the song and adding the accompanying patterns worked on in Section 1 of this unit. Then perform the song with accompaniment (A), your chosen sound piece (B) and then the song with accompaniment again (A). This creates the ABA structure.

Tape record the performance and discuss the effects of the different parts.

Create another ABA sound piece by choosing a different group to play their 'rain' or 'puddle' piece for part B. Tape record this performance.

Ask the children:

- Which sound piece did you prefer?

Encourage the children to try to explain their preferences.

- Which sound piece suited the mood of the song, 'Doctor Foster', better?

Encourage the children to suggest how the choice of instruments may have influenced this.

- What is the main difference between the parts in our ABA piece?

To encourage the children to make suggestions, ask the following questions:

- Can you describe what part A is made up of?
(a song and accompaniment patterns)

- Listen to the sounds – are they tuned or untuned?
(Section A uses tuned percussion instruments and voices singing the tune of Doctor Foster.)

- Can you describe what part B is made up of?
(instrument and body percussion sounds)

- Listen to the sounds – are they tuned or untuned?
(Section B uses untuned percussion instruments and body percussion.)

To conclude, you can explain to the children that the ABA structure of the sound piece is made up of: tuned sounds – part A; untuned sounds - part B; tuned sounds - part A.

Recognising tuned and untuned percussion instruments

Teach the children the following song, on cassette 2, track 4/CD 1, track 30:

Round the circle, round the circle,
When you stop, what will you play?
Round the circle, round the circle,
What will you play?

Answers

1 This can make a high sound.
2 This can make a low sound.
3 This can make just one sound.

Ask the children to sit in a circle. Place the instruments in the middle of the circle and allow each child to choose an instrument, and place it on the floor in front of them.

Tell the children that you are going to play a game in which they are called 'Guardians'. Choose one child and name him the 'Traveller'. The Guardians should sing the song while you lead the child around the circle.

At the end of the song, the Traveller should stop behind one of the Guardians, and pick up the instrument in front of the Guardian. The traveller then plays a sound on the instrument.

The traveller should then decide what kind of sound was made and sing/speak one of the three answers to the song. In the case of an instrument which plays both high and low, e.g. wooden agogo, the child can choose which note to play.

Observation point: Identify those children who are able to tell which instruments can play high and low sounds and which can play only one sound.

The guardian whose instrument was played takes the next turn to be the traveller, and so the game continues.

Creating a sound piece

The children should now be familiar with which instruments are able to produce only one tone, and which instruments can produce more than one tone. They may also have identified those instruments which are able to play more than two tones.

Divide the children into pairs and ask them to work together to create a short sound piece with ABA structure. They should use both tuned and untuned percussion instruments to create both pitched and unpitched sound.

Encourage the children to decide which part will be pitched sound. Remind them that the sound they choose for part A will be repeated.

Support point: If you haven't got enough tuned percussion instruments, let the children use their voices.

Encourage the children to make the B part obviously different to the A part.

When the children have had time to create their short sound piece, ask some of the pairs to play their sounds for the class. Encourage the class to discuss whether the pair have completed the task they have been set. Ask the children:

- Have they created pitched and unpitched sections which sound very different?
- Have they repeated the first section?

If you hear a sound piece and it is difficult to identify where the parts occur, ask the pair to explain how they planned their sequence. This will enable you to identify whether they have understood the activity.

Observation point: Identify those children who show an understanding of pitch and structure.

Section 3

Resources: cassette 2, track 5/CD 1, track 31, cassette 2, track 6/CD 1, track 32, cassette 2, track 7/CD 1, track 33, cassette 2, track 8/CD 1, track 34, cassette 2, track 9/CD 1, track 35, *wooden instruments:* wood-block, wooden agogo, finger castanets; *metal instruments:* triangle, cymbal (tapped with hard beater), cow-bell, indian bells; *skin instruments:* tambour, bongos; *shaking instruments:* multi-guiro, maracas (shaken), cabasa; *scraping instruments:* guiro, multi-guiro (scraped); *tuned percussion instruments:* xylophone/metallophone/glockenspiel/chime bars, notes: F and G

Time guide: 1 hour

Listening

All of the poems and songs in this unit are about water/rain. Play the following extracts: The first, on cassette 2, track 5/CD 1, track 31, is the storm from 'Sheherazade', by Rimsky Korsakoff. You can hear a ship tossing in the sea as it is thrown against the rocks. The second extract, on cassette 2, track 6/CD 1, track 32, is 'Water in Yan River', a Chinese song by Wang Tong-juan, played on the harp. This music conveys the idea of rippling water. The third, cassette 2, track 7/CD 1, track 33, is 'Zuni Pueblo rainbow dance song' – a prayer offering, from New Mexico, to evoke rain.

Performing the rhythm of a poem

Play the children cassette 2, track 8/CD 1, track 34. You will hear the poem, 'Listen to the sound of the gentle falling rain'.

Listen to the sound of the gentle falling rain, (12 claps)
Listen to the sound as it trickles down the pane, (12 claps)
Getting harder, getting wet, (7 claps)
I think I'm going to get upset. (8 claps)
Listen to the sound of the gentle falling rain. (12 claps)

Clap the rhythm of the first line of the poem and ask the children to copy you. You clap the whole poem and allow the children to echo you. Encourage the children to say the words as they clap the rhythm. Repeat any lines that they find difficult. Make sure that everyone is able to clap the rhythm confidently, before you move on. As the children practise clapping, let them clap the first line and you clap the second line, or divide the class into two groups and alternate clapping the lines.

When the children are ready to move on, hand out untuned percussion instruments, and ask them to perform the rhythm of the poem.

Make the performance more interesting by putting the instruments into timbre groups (wooden sounds, metal sounds, shaking and scraping sounds). Divide the children into groups according to the timbre of their instrument and allow the groups to play a line each. The children should continue to speak the words of the poem, no matter which line they are performing. This will help them to play in the right place.

Experiment by changing the order in which the groups play the lines. Ask some groups to play loud sounds and some quiet.

Give out tuned percussion instruments. Allow the children playing the tuned percussion instruments to play the rhythm of the poem on F, while they continue to say the poem. The rest of the class should tap their instruments quietly to the rhythm or, if they are able to do so, they could use their voices, singing the words of the poem on the note F. Perform the poem in this way, taking turns, until most of the children have had sufficient practise on the tuned percussion instruments.

Encourage those children playing an instrument with two tones, e.g. wooden agogo, to perform the rhythm by playing the two sounds alternately. These children should play along with those children using tuned percussion instruments.

Try to allow as many children as possible to play the rhythm of the poem on several instruments.

Singing a Luiseno Indian rain chant

Play cassette 2, track 9/CD 1, track 35. Teach the children the following song:

Breezes are blowing, blowing clouds of water.
Breezes are blowing, blowing clouds of water.
On my face, raining, raining from the ocean.
Breezes are blowing, blowing clouds of water.

When the children are familiar with singing the song gently, ask them to add the following rhythm pattern in accompaniment:

long, short, short
e.g. rub (knees) - long; tap, tap (knees) - short

Play the track again and, without singing, perform the 'long, short, short' rhythm with the song.

Allow some children to play the pattern on drums: rub (skin) - long; tap tap.- short. The rest of the class can sing the song. Next, add to the accompaniment a G, played on a tuned percussion instrument. This note should be played on the steady beat (as indicated by the shaded words). This sound is called a drone.

Extension: If you feel confident about singing, encourage the children to try to hum the G with you, as the child plays the tuned percussion instrument. This hum can be made rhythmically, with the 'long, short, short' rhythm pattern.

Section 4

Resources: cassette 2, track 10/CD 1, track 36, *tuned percussion instruments*: xylophone/glockenspiel/metallophone/chime bars, notes:F, G, A, C, D, a range of untuned percussion instruments

Time guide: 1 hour

Observation point: Identify those children who are able to recognise instruments which are capable of producing more than one tone.

Composing and performing a sound piece

As part of a class discussion, ask the children to collect together all the tuned percussion instruments and instruments which make two tones.

Tell the children that they are going to compose a sound piece with ABA structure. They can use tuned percussion instruments and instruments which make two tones e.g. wooden agogo (which produces pitched sound) for part B. They can use untuned percussion instruments (which produce unpitched sound), for part A.

Divide the children into several groups. Group 1 should use the tuned percussion instruments. They will play part B.

The other groups should use the untuned percussion instruments and be numbered Group 2 onwards. They will take turns to play part A.

Part B: Group 1 will need to use the following notes on the tuned percussion instruments you have available: F, G, A, C, D, F. This is a pentatonic scale starting on F. The children should play the rhythm pattern of the words 'Listen to the sound of the gentle falling rain' on any of those notes.

If you have more than one tuned percussion instrument, suggest that the children with instruments each take a line of the poem and take it in turns to play. Encourage any of the children in this group who are working with two-tone instruments to add a simple ostinato (sound pattern repeated many times). They can do this by repeating the rhythm pattern of the words 'Listen to the sound' over and over again, in the following way: high, high, high, high, low.

Part A: Encourage Groups 2 onwards to create a sound piece using the untuned percussion instruments. In order to link with the theme of the poem, encourage the children to think about the sounds of gentle rain falling, trickling and gradually getting louder as it rains harder. Ask the children to think about how the sounds should start. Ask them:

- Should the sounds be loud/quiet?

Support point: If the time which you had allocated for music comes to an end before all the groups have finished their compositions for part B, encourage the children involved to write down which instruments they were playing, and how. This way, when they continue in the next part, they will know where to start.

- Should the sounds get louder, or quieter, as the rain falls harder?
- Should there be any silences?
- Should all members of the group play together all the time, or join in gradually?
- How should the sound piece end?

When the part A groups are ready, ask them to share their work with the rest of the class and, if possible, tape record their performances. Encourage good listening by asking children not to comment until the sound piece is finished. Encourage structured comments by asking some key questions about the sounds themselves e.g.

- which instrument(s) started to play first?
- Did all of the group play together?
- Which instrument best created the sound of quietly trickling rain?
- Did the music start quietly and get louder?

Observation point: Identify those groups of children who have successfully combined and organised their sounds. Identify those individual children who are able to join in the discussion and talk about the sounds they have heard.

Ask the group performing:

- Did you want the music to be the same loudness throughout?
- Did you want the music to start quietly and end loudly (or vice versa)?
- Do you think you chose the correct instruments for the sounds you wanted?

The children's answers will help you to gain an insight into how much thought went into that group's composition. The questions will give the children an opportunity to appraise and refine their composition.

Try playing part B (Group 1) with part As from different groups and consider which combinations work particularly well. Encourage the children to qualify their preferences. (Remind the groups playing part A to play their sound piece twice, once before Group 1(part B) and once after.

Listening

Play cassette 2, track 10/CD 1, track 36 and listen to 'Rocks and pools'. Ask the children:

- How many parts did the music have?

(three sections)

- What sort of instruments played the first part? (tuned percussion instruments)
- What sort of instruments played the second part? (untuned percussion instruments)
- Can you tell me the structure of the music? (ABA – pitched sound, unpitched sound, pitched sound)

Encourage the children to identify that the music they have heard used the same structure as the sound sequences which they created in the last exercise. Ask the children:
- Can you hear a clear difference between the pitched and unpitched sounds?

Cross-curricular links: Dance

Create movements to the children's composition.

End-of-unit checkpoint:

The children should be able to recognise: tuned percussion instruments produce pitched sound (more than one tone); untuned percussion instruments produce unpitched sound (one tone only). Children should be able to explore, combine and organise pitched and unpitched sounds into a composition with an ABA structure.

Unit 3: Exploring sounds

Main Purpose

to recognise how sounds can be made in different ways, how those sounds can achieve effects and to create music with those sounds

Skills

to listen to and create sounds to achieve effects

Musical Element

Main: Texture, Timbre

Other: Duration, Dynamics

Main Stimuli

Poems for the seasons

Music – 'Spring symphony'

Festivals

Main Activities

- musical games
- singing
- exploring sounds
- creating effects
- responding to recorded music

Activity 1

Exploring timbres of percussion instruments

Purpose:
to develop awareness of the different timbres of tuned and untuned classroom percussion instruments

Resources:
skin instruments: drum, bongo, tambourine; *shaking instruments:* maracas, cabassa, tubo, multi-guiro; *scraping instruments:* guiro,

Ask the children to sit in a circle. Give each child an instrument. Tell them to leave the instruments on the floor until you ask them to play. (If you don't have enough instruments for each child, then give out one between two.)

Ask the children to find two sounds on their instrument. If the children have played this, or similar games, before, ask them:

- How can you alter the way you make a sound?

You can alter the way you play the instrument e.g. scrape/tap guiro; tap cymbal with a beater and cut the sound off by touching the cymbal or let the sound ring; play: loudly/quietly, long/short sounds, high/low sounds.

wooden agogo, multi-guiro (scraped); *metal instruments:* triangle, indian bells, cymbal, jingle bells; *wooden instruments:* wood-block, wooden agogo, castanets, claves; *tuned percussion instruments:* xylophone, chime bars, hand chimes, glockenspiel, metallophone

Time guide:
15–20 minutes

Let the children have a few seconds to experiment with making sounds and at a prearranged signal from you they should stop playing. Hear each child in turn around the circle. The children may play some of the following sounds.

Xylophone/glockenspiel/metallophone: slide beater up or down the bars, play low note/high note; cowbell: hit outside, wiggle beater inside; tambour: rub palm of hand on skin of drum with open hand.

Talk about the sounds that have been made and encourage the children to identify those instruments which make short sounds, those which naturally sustain their sounds (sound keeps going) and those which can play pitched sounds. A wooden agogo has two tones, one high, and one low. It cannot, however, play a tune - it can only play rhythm. A gato drum/slit drum can produce different tones, although it cannot play a tune (within the western scale) either.

Activity 2

Purpose:
to show understanding of the different timbre groups

Resources:
as many instruments as you have available, five cards with labels: 'wooden', 'metal', 'skin', 'shaking', 'scraping'

Time guide:
5 minutes

Sorting instruments according to timbre

Set out your selection of instruments in a random fashion. Display the timbre group cards in 5 different areas of the room. Ask each child to carefully move an instrument from the selection of instruments and put it in its correct timbre group area.

Children may put a metallophone or a cabasa into the wooden instruments group. Remind the children that, although quite a few instruments have wood on them, it is the part of the instrument that is played and produces sound that tells you which group it should go into.

When all of the instruments have been sorted into groups, ask the children to discuss whether the instruments have been sorted into the appropriate places. (You will need to keep the instruments in these groups for Activity 3.)

Activity 3

Purpose:
to develop understanding of the different ways that percussion instruments can be played

Resources:
instruments set out in their timbre groups

Time guide:
15 - 20 minutes

Copying sounds

Divide the children into pairs. Ask both children to choose an instrument, but tell them to each select from a different timbre group to the other one. Set the pairs the following task: one child should copy the sound of the other as closely as possible e.g. child A: wooden agogo – tap, tap, scrape; child B: Maraca – tap, tap, shake.

Ask the children:
- Will it always be possible to copy the sound?

If child A has an instrument which produces a sustaining

sound e.g. cymbal, and child B has an instrument which produces a non-sustaining sound e.g. wood-block, child B will not be able to copy the sound. In this case, child B may decide either that it is impossible for the wood-block to produce a long ringing sound, or that they will represent the long ringing sound by continuing to tap for as long as the ringing sound lasted.

When the children have explored the possibilities for copying, or representing, sounds on different instruments, ask them to talk about what they have found. Encourage them to identify that e.g. pitched sounds on a tuned percussion instrument cannot easily be copied by an untuned percussion instrument, but a two-tone wood-block or wooden agogo might be paired with tuned percussion, in order to copy a high and low sound.

Activity 4

Purpose:
to work co-operatively in small groups, combining sounds from one timbre group; to discuss the effects achieved

Resources:
a selection of tuned and untuned percussion instruments

Time guide:
15 – 20 minutes

Creating a sound piece

Divide the children into small groups. Ask them to create a short sound piece in their group. Each group should create their sound piece using only instruments from a specific timbre group e.g. one group could have all the shaking instruments, another the metal instruments and so on.

Encourage the groups to think about how they can combine their sounds. Ask them to think about how they will start and how they will end their sound piece.

Encourage the groups to share their sound pieces with the rest of the class. Ask the children:

- Which instrument played first?
- How did the piece start?
- Did everyone play all the way through?
- How did the piece make you feel?
- Did any two groups create the same feeling/effect?

Activity 5

Purpose:
to recognise and respond to different timbres

Resources:
cassette 3, track 2/CD 2, track 2

Time guide:
10 minutes

Listening activity

Play 'Scherzo', from Tchaikovsky's 4th symphony, on cassette 3, track 2/CD 2, track 2.

Ask the children to identify which types (timbres) of instruments are playing. First, you will hear the string section playing pizzicato (plucking their strings), then the woodwind section and, finally, the brass section.

The string section of an orchestra normally includes: violin, viola, cello, double bass, harp; the woodwind section includes: piccolo, flute, oboe, clarinet, bassoon; the brass section includes: trumpet, trombone, French horn, tuba.

Activity 6

Purpose:
to begin to show an understanding of timbre and texture

Resources:
a selection of tuned and untuned instruments

Time guide:
15 – 20 minutes

Creating sounds

Divide the children into groups. Ask them to create sounds to represent one of the following:

tide coming in and going out on the shore
ticking clocks
a woodpecker
a steam train

Remind the children to think very carefully about the type (timbre) of instruments they will choose. They should also think about texture - the way in which they are going to combine their chosen sounds.

If a group chooses to create sounds to represent ticking clocks, they will need to play many steady beats, all at different speeds.

If a group chooses to create sounds for a steam train, they will need to consider where the train is travelling and how quickly. They will need to choose a rhythm pattern appropriate to the train's movement.

The groups can share their sound pieces with the rest of the class. Encourage the children to discuss whether groups chose appropriate instruments for the purpose, and whether they combined the sounds well.

Activity 7

Purpose:
to listen to music representing the sounds worked on in Activity 5

Resources:
cassette 3, track 3/CD 2, track 3, cassette 3, track 4/CD 2, track 4

Time guide:
10 minutes

Listening activity

Play the children 'Clock symphony', by Haydn, on cassette 3, track 3/CD 2, track 3.

Ask the children to listen for the steady beat which suggests the ticking of the clock.

Play the children 'John Henry', by Copland, on cassette 3, track 4/CD 2, track 4. This music is written about a train.

Ask the children, as they listen to 'John Henry', to identify the rhythm of the train as it moves across the tracks.

Section 1

Resources: cassette 3, track 5/CD 2, track 5, cassette 3, track 6/CD 2, track 6, cassette 3, track 7/CD 2, track 7, cassette 3, track 8/CD 2, track 8, a range of tuned and untuned percussion instruments

Time guide: 1 hour

The main theme of Sections 1 to 4 in Unit 3, is the seasons. It should be noted that the ideas for Autumn, explored in this Section, can also be applied to the other seasons. The musical elements timbre and texture are the main focus of these units, so particular thought needs to be given to choices of instruments and sounds, and combinations of these.

Singing in a round

Teach the children the song, 'The seasons', with cassette 3, track 5/CD 2, track 5, version 1.

Springtime, summer, autumn, winter,
See the seasons follow on,
Dancing without end.
Always come around again,
Always come around again.

When the children know the song well, encourage them to sing it as a round. There are several ways to do this - first, ask them to say the words of the song, rhythmically. When they have done this, divide the class into two groups, and let Group 1 say the song first. Group 2 should start saying the song when the first group reaches the word 'see' at the beginning of line 2.

When the children are able to speak the round confidently, play cassette 3, track 6/CD 2, track 6, 'The seasons',version 2. Let the tape perform as Group 1, the class as Group 2 and sing the song as a round.

When the class are familiar with this activity, use version 2 of 'The seasons' as Group 1 and *sing* the song as a two part round. With greater confidence, the children can go on to sing a three part round.

A different effect can be achieved by performing the song in the following way. Divide the class into three groups. Play cassette 3, track 7/CD 2, track 7, 'The seasons', version 3. Group 1 should start by singing the first line. They should keep repeating it over and over again. After they have sung it three times, bring in Group 2 with the second and third lines which they keep repeating. You should now have the groups singing their words simultaneously. After Group 2 have sung three times, bring in Group 3 with the fourth line.

Encourage the children to listen carefully while they are performing, to make sure that they sing in time together.

Creating a sound piece for autumn

Encourage the children to suggest descriptive words on the theme of autumn, and write some of their words on the board. They may identify: wind, rain, decaying leaves, falling leaves, changing colours and so on. Ask the children to describe autumnal leaves. Encourage them to identify words such as: 'crisp', 'fluttering', 'whirling', 'spinning', 'scrunch'.

As a class, decide on a 'storyboard' for your autumn sounds e.g. firstly the wind blows the leaves from the trees. Secondly, the leaves fall to the ground. Thirdly, someone brushes the leaves up off the ground. Lastly, the leaves fall again.

For this 'storyboard', there are three main actions, and you could divide the class into three groups to play these sounds.

Ask the children:
• What sort of sounds do you think you will need to create music for leaves moving in the wind and falling?
Encourage them to identify scraping sounds, wooden sounds, shaking sounds, gentle sounds or specific instruments which make some of these sounds e.g. guiro, cabasa.

Ask the children:
• What sort of sounds do you think you will need to create music for the wind in the trees?
Encourage them to identify vocal sounds, shaking sounds, gentle sounds or specific instruments e.g. drum skin (rubbed).

Observation point: Identify those children who are able to make appropriate and interesting suggestions for sounds. Also, identify those children who are beginning to remember the names of instruments.

• Will you choose tuned or untuned instruments to create music for the leaves being brushed away?
Encourage them to identify untuned sounds e.g. shaking and scraping sounds played on maracas (gently shaken)/guiro (quietly scraped).

• Will the sounds for leaves falling down get higher or lower? (The pitch of sounds should get lower, as the leaves fall down.)

• Will the sounds be loud, or quiet?

• Will you play the sounds rhythmically or freely?

Ask the children to create sounds in their groups. Remind them to choose instruments which will be appropriate for the sounds which they are trying to create. Encourage them to think about, and discuss, how they should start and stop their music and what order they should play their sounds in.

Ask the children:
• Will you play all at once, separately, or in specific combinations?
• Will you play loudly/quietly, fast/slow?

Support point: The children should make a record, either written or using graphic notation, of the sounds and instruments and the sequence of sounds which they have chosen. This will be useful if they have to stop composing and continue on another occasion.

Those children who find it difficult to identify what to play can choose one of the descriptive autumn words written on the board earlier. They can play the rhythm of that word on their chosen instrument. This is a useful exercise in other compositions which the children may create.

Listen to all the children's pieces and then allow them to play them in the sequence of the storyboard. Tape record the results and allow the children to listen to the sounds and talk about how they can be improved.

Listening

Play the children cassette 3, track 8/CD 2, track 8. Ask them to listen to the vocal music about autumn. 'Fly, fly, fly' is a piece of music which reflects the falling of leaves. It is sung as a round.

Section 2

Resources: cassette 3, track 9/CD 2, track 9, cassette 3, track 10/CD 2, track 10, cassette 3, track 11/CD 2, track 11, a selection of tuned and untuned percussion instruments

Time guide: 1 hour

Creating sounds for summer

Play the children 'Yellow', a poem about summer, on cassette 3, track 9/CD 2, track 9. Ask them to listen carefully to the words.

Yellow and mellow,
Warm now and stretched,
Lengthily stretched
On yellow–gold sand.
And sleepily smiling,
Smile like a flower,
Basking and kind
And mightily purring,
A cat in the sunlight,
On newly-mown grass,
Green, green, grass.

Ask the children to suggest which words made them think about summer. Encourage them to identify how the poem made them feel – lazy, warm, comfortable, relaxed, sleepy?

Encourage the children to think about whether the poem tells a story (with a beginning, middle and end), describes a picture, or whether it simply suggests lots of different images and feelings (about sunshine, sand, a flower, a cat, grass).

Play the poem 'End of summer' on cassette 3, track 10/CD 2, track 10.

Observation point: Identify those children who respond and are able to talk about how the poem made them feel.

Swimming,
Building castles
Out of sand at the shore,
Till the tide comes washing away
Summer.

Ask the children:
• How did the poem make you feel?

Ask the children to compare the two poems:
• Does one poem describe more activity than the other?
Encourage the children to notice that 'Yellow' describes lengthily stretching, sleepily smiling, purring. 'End of summer' describes swimming, building castles, the tide washing in.

Ask the children to talk about the things and feelings which they associate with summer. As in Section 1, you can write some of the words they use on the board e.g. heat, sunshine, seaside and so on.

Play cassette 3, track 9/CD 2, track 9, and listen to 'Yellow' again. Ask the children:
• What sort of sounds would you use to make summer music for this poem?
Encourage them to identify slow, relaxing sounds, rather than loud, fast, lively sounds.

• What sort of instruments would you need to make the sounds?
Encourage them to identify instruments which make long (sustaining) sounds e.g. metallophone, glockenspiel, cymbals, indian bells.

As in Section 1, if some children find it difficult to find the right sounds, let them choose words from the poem and think about how to play these individually e.g. long, slow scrapes on the guiro for 'lengthily stretched', or glocken-spiel/bells for 'smile like a flower'.

Play cassette 3, track 10/CD 2, track 10, and listen to 'End of summer' again. Ask the children:
• What could you use to make water sounds for the swimming and splashing and the tide washing in?
• What sounds could you use for building sandcastles?

Encourage the children to identify building up their sounds and making patterns of sounds, one layer at a time.

Ask the children to work in groups, some should work on creating sounds to convey the atmosphere of 'Yellow' and some should convey the atmosphere of 'End of summer'. The children should not say the words of the poem as they perform their sounds - the poem acts as a stimulus and helps to give order and shape to the sound piece and the exercise. The children can share their results with the class and tape record their music.

Ask the children to assess and discuss how or whether the sounds and instruments, chosen by the different groups, combined to convey the mood of the poem.

Extension: Encourage the children to write their own poems to use as stimuli for creating music. The children can be encouraged to create sounds to convey the mood of the words.

Listening

Play listening extracts which create a 'lazy summer' mood and atmosphere e.g. 'Summertime', by George Gershwin on cassette 3, track 11/CD 2, track 11.

The slow tempo of the music, combined with the long notes and the lazy style of the melody that the soloist sings, help to suggest a long, hot summer's day when everyone needs to move slowly, in order to stay cool.

Cross-curricular links: Art

Look at paintings related to the seasons of the year e.g. for winter, Monet's 'Winter in Vetheuil', 'Break up of ice, Lavercourt', 'Sunshine and snow, Lavercourt,' and Breugel the elder's 'Hunters in the snow'. For autumn, 'Autumn leaves', by John Everett Millais. For summer, Seurat's 'The bather' and 'Sunday afternoon on the Grand Jette'. For spring, 'Early spring', by John William Inchbold, or 'Spring at Giverny', by Monet.

Encourage the children to draw/paint pictures to go with the listening extracts or their own compositions.

Section 3

Resources: cassette 3, track 12/CD 2, track 12, cassette 3, track 13/CD 2, track 13, cassette 3, track 14/CD 2, track 14, a selection of tuned and untuned percussion instruments

Time guide: 1 hour

Listen to the short musical extract, about spring, on cassette 3, track 12/CD 2, track 12. Explain that this is from 'The spring symphony', by Benjamin Britten, an English composer who died in 1976. Explain that the music is set to a poem by Thomas Nashe, who died in 1601. The poem begins with the words 'Spring, the sweet spring, is the year's pleasant king'. The music has a happy swinging rhythm as spring is being welcomed in.

Ask the children:
- What did you notice about the extract?

Encourage them to identify that they heard voices and an orchestra.

- Could you hear a man singing, a woman singing, or both? (They should identify both male and female voices.)
- What were the sounds of spring that you heard? (bird sounds: jug-jug, pu-we, to-witta-woo, cuckoo calling)
- What made the bird sounds – voices or instruments? (voices)

Creating a sound piece for spring

Music created for this season can build upon the theme of spring as a time of growth. You can also link spring, if you wish to do so, with the festival of Easter.

Ask the children to suggest words which remind them of spring e.g. 'growth', 'awakening', 'nest-building', 'showers', 'seeds', 'buds', 'green'.

'The spring Symphony', on cassette 3, track 12/CD 2, track 12, is the stimulus for this activity.

Talk to the children about some bird calls which can be heard in spring. They may copy bird calls from 'The spring symphony'. Ask the children to try to make some of the sounds, using their voices. (If the class make the sounds together, use a pre-arranged signal to ensure they start and stop when you wish.) Allow the children to experiment by putting some of the different bird calls together.

Ask the children to find different instruments which are capable of making bird sounds e.g. the cuckoo's call can be played on a metallophone (C followed by lower A); the woodpecker's tapping can be played on the wood-block; make varied bird sounds by alternating quickly between two notes on a glockenspiel. (Often children will need to use vocal sounds to produce bird calls.)

Allow the children to work in groups. They should create a sound piece of bird calls, using instruments and voices. When they have composed their pieces, each group should share their music with the class. Tape record the children's compositions.

Encourage the children, in their groups, to create spring music. They should think about how to make their sounds grow, to reflect growth as the main theme for spring: music should build up gradually – one person begins playing, slowly others join in one at a time; play low notes, on tuned percussion instruments, gradually getting higher.

The children should think about the mood of spring when they play. Ask the children to think about the happy welcoming music of 'The spring symphony'. Children can think of short phrases for spring and play the rhythm of those words e.g. 'Welcome to spring', 'Spring is here, Hallelujah!'

When the children have composed their pieces, each group should share their music with the class again. Tape record the children's compositions.

Encourage the children to create their own spring symphony by interspersing the bird call sounds with the 'growing' music.

Listening

Listen to the following extracts of spring music. Play cassette 3, track 13/CD 2, track 13, 'The rite of spring' by Stravinsky, a Russian composer who died in 1971. The music was first written for a ballet and is about a pagan rite for welcoming the spring. It sounds very different to 'The spring symphony', as there are no voices. An orchestra plays the rhythmic music. The second extract is from 'On hearing the first cuckoo in spring', by Delius, on cassette 3, track 14/CD 2, track 14.

Encourage the children to identify the sound of the cuckoo, which occurs in the music several times. Encourage the children to try to identify also the instrument which is playing this sound. The sound is played by the clarinet.

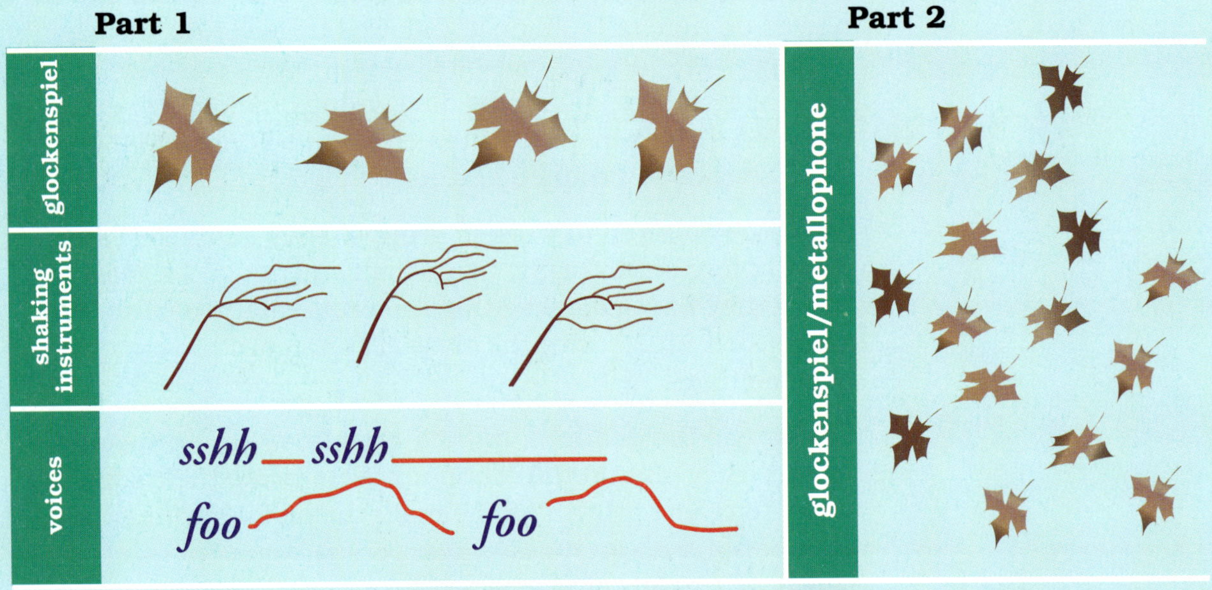

Extension: Encourage the children to create their own form of notation to record some of the compositions they have so far created e.g. autumn sounds could be represented by pictures of leaves falling/wind blowing. The notation shows which instruments are played and the order in which they are played.

Part 1: the sounds of leaves falling, played on the glockenspiel, the sounds of wind blowing through the trees, played on shaking instruments and with vocal sounds.

Part 2: the sounds of leaves falling, played on the glockenspiel and metallophone.

Section 4

Resources: cassette 3, track 15/CD 2, track 15, cassette 3, track 16/CD 2, track 16, cassette 3, track 17/CD 2, track 17, cassette 3, track 18/CD 2, track 18, cassette 3, track 19/CD 2, track 19, cassette 3, track 20/CD 2, track 20, cassette 3, track 21/CD 2, track 21, copymasters 1, 8, 9, 10 and 11 xylophone/metallophone/chime bars, notes: C and G, indian bells, drum, cymbal

Time guide: 1 hour

Where: the hall

There are many festivals which take place in winter and spring: winter festivals e.g. Christmas, New Year, Chinese New Year, Holi (Hindu), Divali (Hindu), Chanukah (Jewish), Shrove Tuesday; spring festivals e.g. Easter, Harvest, Pesach/Passover (Jewish).

Chinese New Year

Play the 'Fenyang flower drum song', (version 1) on cassette 3, track 15/CD 2, track 15. Teach the children the song.

Verse
Fenyang flower drum
Fenyang flower drum
Let's play the tune as we sing this song.
And as we sing the Fenyang flower drum song
Let's play the tune on our drum and gong.

Chorus
Drum, drum, drum, piao – m – piao.
Drum, drum, drum, piao – m – piao.
Drum, piao, drum, piao,
Drum, piao, piao, piao, piao, – m – piao.

Allow the children to sing the song several times, until they are familiar with it.

Explain to the children that Chinese New Year is the most important festival in the Chinese year. It takes place between january and february and lasts for fifteen days. The colour red is used frequently for decoration and clothing, as it is traditionally considered to be very lucky.

Add a drone:
Play the track and ask one child to play a drone on the notes G and (lower) C on the underlined words only. This produces a pattern of 'taa, saa, taa, saa'. Explain to the children that 'saa' means 'silence'.

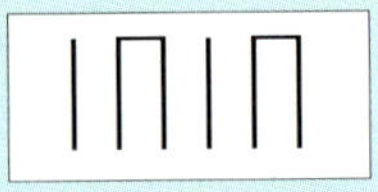
8

Observation point:
Identify those children who are able to clap this rhythm.

Support point:
When children are playing indian bells, encourage them to hold one bell still and hit the other with it.

1

9

Add an ostinato:
Encourage the children to clap the pattern of the flashcard made from copymaster 8.

The children can say, 'taa, ta – tay, taa, ta – tay', to help them keep the rhythm pattern. Without singing, the children should clap this rhythm.

Choose between two and four children, depending on how many instruments you have, and ask half of them to play the flashcard rhythm pattern on indian bells. They should play this with the verse. Ask the other half of the selected children to play the flashcard rhythm pattern on a drum, during the chorus.

Play version 2 of the song, on cassette 3, track 16/CD 2, track 16, and allow the children to perform the flashcard to accompany the track. The rest of the children should sing the song. If the children are performing confidently, play the song again and add the drone accompaniment.

Add a drum sound and a gong sound:
Choose two more children. One should play the steady beat on a drum, during the verse - see the steady beat flashcard on copymaster 1. The second child should perform the pattern on a flashcard made from copymaster 9. This should be played on a gong or cymbal during the chorus only. They should say the words 'taa, saa, taa, saa', in their heads, to help them keep time. (Explain that 'saa' means rest/silence.)

Sing the song again with version 2 on the cassette/CD and add the steady beat on the drum and the rhythm pattern on the gong/cymbal, as an accompaniment.

Deciding on an accompaniment:
Ask the children to think about how they would like the accompaniment to sound and consider which combination of sounds (i.e. texture) they prefer. Encourage them to experiment to find out e.g. they may decide to let all the ideas for accompaniment sounds play together throughout, or they may choose to play certain accompaniments only in the verse and some in the chorus e.g.

Verse

indian bells

8 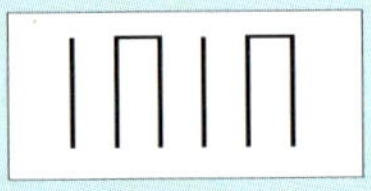

(taa, ta-tay, taa, ta-tay)

drum

1 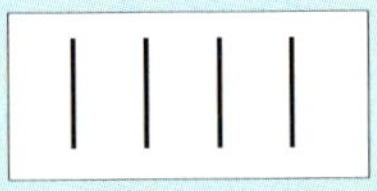

(steady beat)

C and G

9 

(drone-taa, saa, taa, saa)

chorus

drum

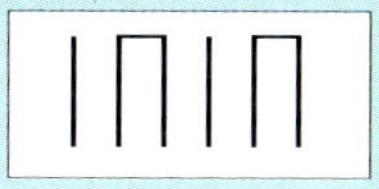

8

(taa, ta-tay, taa, ta-tay)

cymbal/gong

9

(drone – taa, saa, taa, saa)

C and G

9

(drone – taa, saa, taa, saa)

Listening

Listen to some more winter music: 'Antartica', by Vaughan Williams, is on cassette 3, track 17/CD 2, track 17. Listen for the wind sounds (these are made by a wind machine) and talk about the other sound effects used to create the feeling of cold and ice.

'Footsteps in the snow', by Debussy, is another winter piece, on cassette 3, track 18/CD 2, track 18.

Listen to 'Troika' by Prokofiev, on cassette 3, track 19/CD 2, track 19. Ask the children to listen to the jingle of the bells on the sleigh depicted through the music, as it is pulled along in the snow.

The following listening materials are related to festivals from around the world: 'Party tonight', on cassette 3, track 20/ CD 2, track 20. This celebrates Carnival, and is played on Caribbean steel drums. 'Yu da ba jiao', on cassette 3, track 21/ CD 2, track 21, is a piece of Chinese music which can be played at New Year celebrations.

End-of-unit checkpoint:

The children should be able to: recognise how sounds can be made in different ways; recognise how particular sounds and combinations of sounds (timbres) can achieve effects; create music using different sounds and combinations of sounds (timbres); create music with different textures, to achieve effects.

Unit 4: Building up sounds

Main Purpose

to play simple accompaniment patterns when singing, to be aware of dynamics: loud/quiet, getting louder/quieter

Skills

to sing and play accompaniments and control dynamics of sounds

Musical Element

Main: Dynamics

Other: Timbre, Texture, Duration

Main Stimuli

Song – 'Tshiyoyo'

Main Activities

- musical games
- singing
- exploring sounds
- creating effects
- responding to recorded music

Activity 1

Purpose:
to develop awareness and control of dynamics (loud/quiet)

Resources:
flashcards with labels (see Activity)

Time guide:
10–15 minutes

Loud and quiet game using vocal and body percussion

You will need to produce a set of cards with the following labels. It is useful to write the instructions on both sides of the card, so that you do not have to turn the card around.

- tap your table top **quietly**
- stamp one foot **loudly** once
- say 'rrr' **quietly**
- make a **loud** sound
- rub your hands together **quietly**
- stamp your feet **loudly**

Hold up each card in turn, to check that the children can read and understand what each one says, and so that they can practise making each sound.

Extension: Allow the children to make up their own loud

and quiet cards with short simple instructions on them, for the class to use. They can do this individually, in pairs, or as a small group activity.

Activity 2

Purpose:
to control loud and quiet body percussion sounds

Time guide:
10–15 minutes

Loud and quiet game

Ask the children to sit in a circle. Start the activity by making one loud clap. Each child sitting in the circle should take turns to do this, until the sound reaches you again. This time, make one quiet clap for the children to copy.

Vary this by making: two loud claps; two quiet claps; one loud clap, followed by one quiet clap. Alternatively, use any vocal, or body percussion, sound with which the children are familiar. When the children are more confident with the activity, allow individual children to lead the activity.

Activity 3

Purpose:
to control loud and quiet sounds on percussion instruments

Resources:
maracas, tambour, wood-block, chime bar, guiro, tambourine, drum, flashcards with labels (see Activity)

Time guide:
20–25 minutes

Loud and quiet game using percussion instruments

Make flashcards with the following labels. (If you don't have any of the instruments, adapt the flashcards accordingly.)

- shake a maraca **quietly**
- play a tambour **loudly** with your hand
- tap a wood-block **quietly** three times
- shake two maracas **loudly**
- play a chime bar **quietly**
- make **quiet** sounds on a guiro
- make a **loud** sound on a tambourine
- make two **loud** sounds on a drum

Without showing the rest of the class, give the cards to eight different children (or fewer, if you prefer).

Allow the selected children to choose a percussion instrument which is appropriate to their card. Each child should then make the appropriate loud or quiet sound. The task for the rest of the class is to guess what it said on the player's card. (This activity can also be done in pairs or small groups.) Repeat the activity allowing different children to play the instruments.

Extension: Encourage the children to create their own loud and quiet cards, to be used in the same way. The cards can represent: body percussion sounds, vocal sounds, percussion instrument sounds, environmental sounds or any combination of these. It is important that each instruction that the children create should have 'quietly'/ 'quiet' or 'loudly'/ 'loud' written on it.

Observation point:
Identify those children who are able to control making loud and quiet sounds on their instruments.

Activity 4

Purpose:
to control loud and quiet sounds on a range of percussion instruments

Resources:
a range of percussion instruments

Time guide:
15 minutes

Loud and quiet game using percussion instruments

This game is played in the same way as Activity 2. Make a loud/quiet sound on a percussion instrument and each child around the circle should take turns to copy the sound. If you do not have enough instruments for every child, ask the children to get into pairs and take turns to play the instrument. Repeat the activity so that both children take a turn.

Activity 5

Purpose:
to play loud and quiet sounds, from symbols, using body percussion and percussion instruments

Resources:
copymasters 12, 13, 14, 15, 16, 17, a selection of untuned percussion instruments

Time guide:
15 – 20 minutes

12 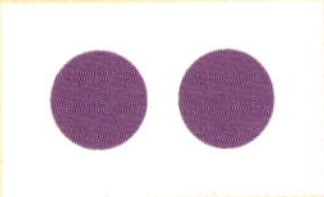

13 

14 

15 

16 

17 

Playing loud and quiet sounds from symbols

Make flashcards from copymasters 12 and 13.

Hold up the flashcard made from copymaster 12. Ask the children:

- How would you play this card?

(Make two loud sounds.)

Hold up the flashcard made from copymaster 13 and ask the same question – the answer should be two quiet sounds.

Choose one of the following prearranged signals for the children to begin: count ‘1, 2, 3, 4’, or say ‘and’. This allows the children to start together. Listen to whether they all played two loud sounds followed by two quiet sounds.

Hold up the first flashcard again and ask the children to make two loud claps. Hold up the second flashcard and ask the children to make two quiet claps.

Use copymasters 14, 15, 16, 17, to make flashcards.

Hold up each flashcard in turn, and ask the children to clap the pattern on the card, as you run your fingers slowly along the symbols from left to right.

Repeat the activity, using the flashcards. This time, the children should make the loud and quiet sounds using percussion instruments.

Activity 6

Purpose:
to control sounds gradually getting louder and gradually getting quieter

Resources:
tambour, a range of percussion instruments

Time guide:
15–20 minutes

Controlling loud and quiet sounds

Draw the following sequence of symbols on the board.

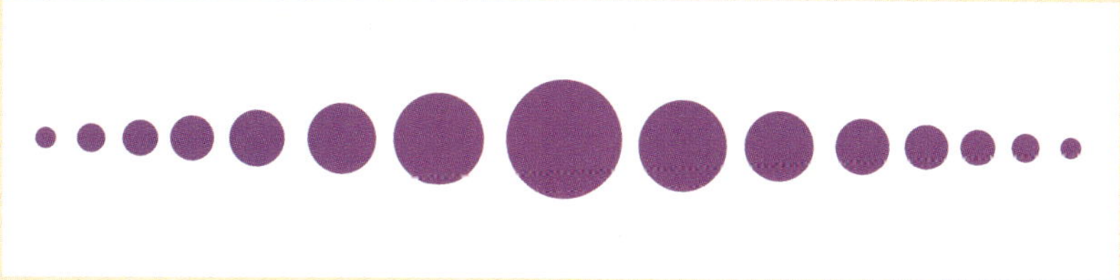

Point to each symbol and ask the children to perform the pattern by clapping. Make sure that the children perform their quiet claps quietly enough, and don't get loud too soon. Ask if someone would like to try playing the sequence on a tambour.

Encourage the children to perform the pattern on various percussion instruments.

Try to perform the pattern as a whole class. Talk about which instruments are better for playing the sounds.

Extension: In small groups, let the children create a sequence of loud, quiet, and gradually louder and quieter sounds.

Encourage them to draw/write, to record their sounds for another group to play.

Activity 7

Purpose:
to create symbols for loud and quiet sounds

Resources:
cassette 4, track 2/CD 2, track 22

Time guide
10–15 minutes

Listening activity

Listen to, 'Dynamics'. As they listen, the children can draw a picture to reflect the music, using the symbols with which they are familiar i.e. big circles for loud sounds, little circles for quiet sounds and circles getting larger or smaller e.g.

Section 1

Resources: cassette 4, track 3/CD 2, track 23, cassette 4, track 4/CD 2, track 24, copymasters 18, 19, 26, 2 or 3 F chime bars/notes on alto metallophone

Time guide: 1 hour

Singing 'Tshiyoyo'

Play 'Tshiyoyo' on cassette 4, track 3/CD 2, track 23.

1 Look at those birds, flapping their wings,
2 Ziphaphazela, ziphaphazela.
3 They sing 'tshiyoyo', they sing 'tshiyoyo',
4 They sing 'tshiyoyo, ziphaphazela'.

Play the song again and ask the children to listen for the words that are repeated. Play the song a third time and, this time, ask the children to clap the rhythm of the song.

The rhythm pattern for each line in 'Tshiyoyo' is the same: 'short, short, short, long, long.' The children should say 'ziphaphazela', as they clap.

When the children are confident with clapping the rhythm of the words and the rhythm pattern, ask them to replace the clapping with a different body percussion sound for each line: line 1 – pat chest, line 2 – tap fingers, line 3 – pat knees, line 4 – clap hands.

By now, the children should be more familiar with 'Tshiyoyo'. Play the song again and encourage the children to try to sing along with the song.

Observation point: Identify those children who are able to perform the drone successfully.

Adding a simple accompaniment pattern to 'Tshiyoyo'

Explain to the children that they are going to add a drone to the song. Give the F chime bars and/or metallophone to two or three children. Encourage the children to add an F at the beginning of each new phrase. The beginning of each phrase is indicated by the shaded words.

Listening

Listen to some gentle music played on a mbira (thumb piano) on cassette 4, track 4/CD 2, track 24. The piece is called 'Safari na muziki'. The thumb piano used in this extract has 66 metal tongues which are plucked by thumbs and forefingers.

Getting louder, getting quieter

18

19

Make flashcards from copymasters 18 and 19 and introduce the children to the symbols.

Ask the children:
- What do the symbols represent?

(18. getting gradually louder, 19. getting gradually quieter)

Demonstrate the first flashcard, slowly trace your finger along the card from left to right and, as you do so, start patting your knee quietly and gradually get louder as you move further towards the right. With the second flashcard, make your knee patting get gradually quieter as you move your finger from left to right. Display the two flashcards together, trace the line from left to right on the first card, gradually making louder pats, then repeat the action on the second card, gradually making your knee patting quieter again.

The storm – performing quiet and loud sounds

Ask the children to sit in a circle. Explain to them that you are going to pass body percussion sounds around the circle. The first child will continue to make the sound when the second child begins making it and so on. This way, the sounds will gradually accumulate as each new child starts performing.

Start by rubbing your hands together. Invite each child around the circle to copy you, and continue with this sound until, eventually, every child in the circle is making the same sound as you.

Change your sound to finger tapping. Until it is their turn to begin finger tapping, each child should continue to rub hands together. This way, some children will be finger tapping and some still rubbing hands. Change your sound again, to knee tapping and, finally, to foot stamping. (At each sound change, some children will always still be making the previous sound.)

Follow this by reversing the body percussion sounds: firstly, pat knees, secondly, tap fingers and thirdly, rub hands.

Try to ensure that the body percussion sounds are kept continuous and overlapping. This way, you will achieve a graduation of sounds from quiet to loud and quiet again.

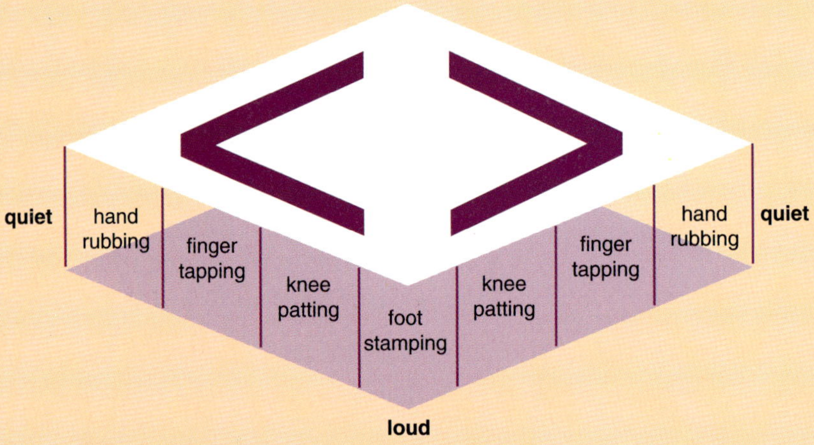

Ask the children:
- What happened to the sound?
(They should answer that the sounds get louder and then quieter.)

- Which was the loudest sound?
(foot stamping)

- Which was the quietest sound?
(hand rubbing)

Section 2

Resources: cassette 4, track 3/CD 2, track 23, cassette 4, track 5/CD 2, track 25, cassette 4, track 6/CD 2, track 26, cassette 4, track 7/CD 2, track 27, *untuned percussion instruments:* wood-block, maracas, tambourine, drum/tambour, cowbell, cabasa; *tuned percussion instruments:* alto metallophone/chime bars, notes: F and C

Time guide: 1 hour

Opposite sounds

The following exercise requires the children to use body percussion to echo sounds which you make. The children will need to think about how to perform a dynamically opposite sound:

Clap a short pattern e.g. 'short, short, long, short, short, long,' saying the words as you clap. Make sure you clap loudly. The children should clap the same pattern, but they should make sure they clap quietly.

When the children are confident about the exercise, allow individuals to lead.

Adding accompaniment patterns to 'Tshiyoyo'

Play 'Tshiyoyo' on cassette 4, track 3/CD 2, track 23. Encourage the children to sing along with the track. Repeat this until the children are again familiar with the song.

Choose two or three children to play the rhythm pattern of the song on untuned percussion instruments. The rhythm pattern ('short, short, short, long, long') should be played on each line. The children can say 'Ziphaphazela' repeatedly, to help them to maintain the pattern.

Sing the song again, with the track, and add this rhythmic accompaniment. Add the drone played on F, as in Section 1.

You should now have three layers of sound: the song, the drone accompaniment, the rhythmic accompaniment.

Performing loud and quiet rhythms from symbols

Display any one of the flashcards you have which uses the large dot to represent loud sounds and the small dot to represent quiet sounds. Ask the children:

Can anyone remember how to clap this?

Display the following matrix of sounds. using flashcards made from copymasters 26 and 10.

drum/tambour

26 10

cowbell

cabasa

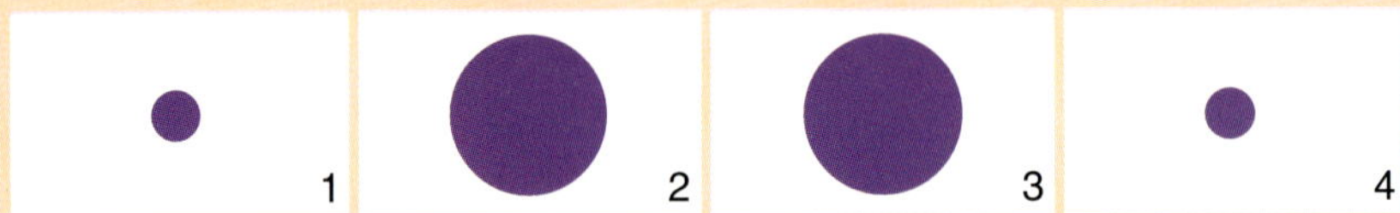

claves

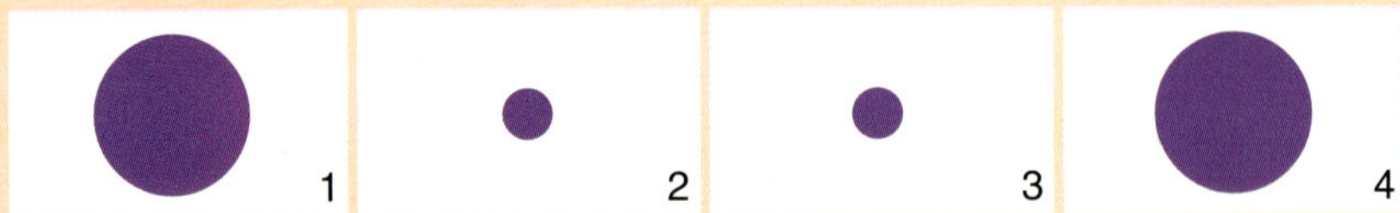

Support point:
Each numbered square is equivalent to one steady beat.

Encourage the children to perform the matrix firstly by clapping, so that they become familiar with the sequence of symbols e.g. line one – clap loudly, clap quietly, clap loudly, clap quietly.

They should try to allow each line to follow on, so that the sounds are played as a continuous steady beat.

When the children are confident about clapping the patterns with a steady beat, allow them to take turns in performing the symbols on the instruments.

Next, allow the child playing the drum/tambour line, and the child playing the cowbell, to play their lines together. Count '1, 2, 3, 4', for the children to begin playing together. If this is successful, let the children playing the cabasa and claves also play together. You can follow this by allowing all four children to play together. Remind the children to clearly differentiate their loud and quiet sounds. The rest of the class should listen to check whether the sounds are performed accurately, according to the matrix.

Performing rhythms for 'Way way, the lion'

Play 'Way way, the lion' (version 1) on cassette 4, track 5/CD 2, track 25. Ask the children to listen to the loud and quiet sounds accompanying the song. Encourage them to identify that they are the same as they played in the last exercise.

Play the children 'Way way, the lion' (version 2) on cassette 4, track 6/CD 2, track 26. Allow the children to perform, from the matrix of symbols in the last exercise, with the track.

If there are enough instruments, you can allow two or three children to perform each line. (It will be important, in this case, to ensure that the children do play the quiet sound symbols quietly.)

Repeat the activity, allowing more children the chance to perform.

Extension: Teach the children the song, 'Way way, the lion'. The song is on version 3, cassette 4, track 7/CD 2, track 27.

Way, way, oh way, oh the lion,
Pass a pebble, pass a pebble, pass a pebble on.

Observation point: Identify those children who are able to continue playing their pattern while the song is sung.

The children can perform the loud and quiet matrix on the drum/tambour, cowbell, cabasa, claves, with this version of the song.

A drone on the note C can be added as an accompaniment. This should be played on the shaded words, as indicated.

Allow the children to make their own matrix of sounds, using their own choice of instruments.

Section 3

Resources: cassette 4, track 8/CD 2, track 28, cassette 4, track 9/CD 2, track 29, cassette 4, track 10/CD 2, track 30, cassette 4, track 11/CD 2, track 31, cassette 4, track 12/CD 2, track 32, *tuned percussion instruments:* chime bars/metallophone/ xylophone, notes: C, E, F, G, A, C

Time guide: 1 hour

Opposite sounds

Clap the rhythm pattern for 'Tshiyoyo' (short, short, short, long, long) loudly. The children should echo your rhythm pattern, but clap quietly.

Speak the word 'Ziphaphazela', loudly. The children should repeat the word quietly.

Sing the word 'Ziphaphazela', quietly. The children should sing the word back to you, loudly.

Support point:
Sing quietly or loudly, so that the children can identify that they should sing in the opposite way.

Adding an accompaniment pattern to 'Tshiyoyo'

The following accompaniment patterns for tuned percussion instruments can be added to 'Tshiyoyo' on the following lines:

1	Look	at	those	bi	–	rds
	<u>F</u>		<u>F</u>			<u>F</u>
		<u>C</u>		<u>C</u>		

3	They	sing	Tshi –	yo	–	yo
	<u>C^1</u>	<u>C^1</u>	<u>C^1</u>	<u>C^1</u>		
						<u>A</u>

> **Support point:**
> When a short pattern, like those in this exercise, are repeated continuously, this is called an 'ostinato'. In this case, the patterns have pitched sounds or notes and are called melodic (or tuned) ostinato.

4	Zi –	pha –	pha –	ze –	la
			G		
	F	F			F
				E	

These patterns all have the same rhythm so that each one of the three patterns can be played throughout the song. Alternatively, the patterns can be played at once, to accompany the song.

Those children not playing instruments should continue to sing the song.

Singing 'Mumma warrano'

Play 'Mumma warrano', version 1, on cassette 4, track 8/CD 2, track 28. Teach the children the song.

Mumma warrano, murra wathano,
Mumma warrano, murra wathano,
Mumma warrano, murra wathano,
Mumma warrano, murra wathano,
Mmmm ______, mmmm ______,
Mmmm ______, murra wathano.

This is an Aboriginal song. It comes from the Maranoa district of Queensland, Australia.

Encourage the children to identify the purpose for which the song is intended, as a lullaby. You can ask certain leading questions:

- Why do you think this song is a quiet song?
- Who do you think it might be sung to?

When the children are able to sing the song confidently, allow them to add a quiet simple sound in accompaniment at the beginning of each new phrase in the song (indicated by the shaded words).

The following are some ideas for accompaniments for you to use: play F on chime bar/metallophone/glockenspiel; play one sound on indian bells. (On version 2 of the song, on cassette 4, track 9/CD 2, track 29, you can hear these two accompaniments.)

Listening

Listen to the following extracts of music. The first, on cassette 4, track 10/CD 2, track 30, is taken from 'The organ concerto' by Poulenc. This piece contains both loud and quiet sounds. The second extract, on cassette 4, track 11/CD 2, track 31, 'I surrender' contains loud sounds played by a rock band. The third extract, on cassette 4, track 12/CD 2, track 32, 'Samba triste', contains quiet sounds played on an acoustic guitar. Although guitars are used in both of the last two extracts, they create totally different sounds and effects.

Section 4

Resources: cassette 4, track 13/CD 2, track 33, cassette 4, track 3/CD 2, track 23, cassette 4, track 14/CD 2, track 34, *untuned percussion instruments:* tambour, wood-block, gato/slit drum; *tuned percussion instruments:* chime bars/xylophone, notes: D, E, F, A, B

Time guide: 1 hour

The storm – playing percussion instruments

Create the storm effect, from Section 2 of this unit, again, this time using percussion instruments and graphic notation (symbols for sounds). The following are some ideas for you to use:

body percussion sound	graphic symbols	represents	untuned percussion instrument
hand rubbing	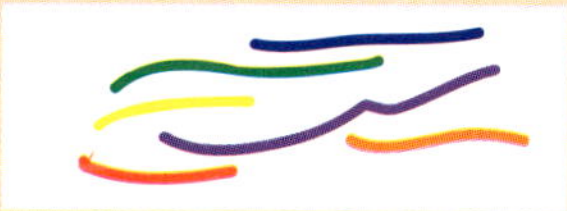	wind	rub tambour/ drum skin
finger tapping	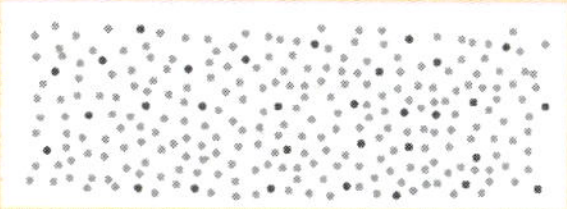	gentle rain	tap fingers on tambour; hit wood-block randomly
knee patting		heavy rain	gato drum; D, E, F, A, B on xylophone
foot stamping		downpour & thunder	beat drums & tambour with beaters

Replace hand rubbing with rubbing tambour/drum. This can represent the wind. Create a symbol/flashcard to represent this sound e.g.

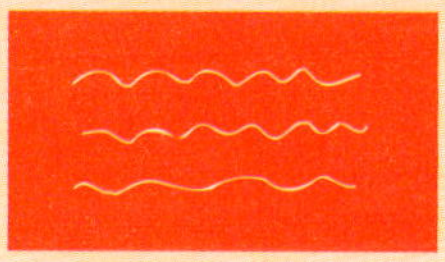

or

Replace finger tapping with tapping beaters on tambour, drum or wood-block. This can represent gentle rain. Create a symbol/flashcard to represent this sound e.g.

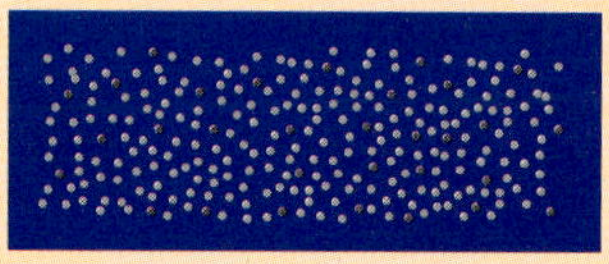

Replace knee patting with xylophone notes D, E, F, A, B.

This can represent the heavy rain precipitating the storm. Create a symbol/flashcard to represent this sound e.g.

Replace foot stamping with beating drums and tambours with beaters. This can represent the downpour and thunder of the storm. Create a symbol/flashcard to represent this sound e.g.

You can organise the exercise in the following way: Divide the children sitting in the circle into four groups. Allocate a storm sound and the instruments on which to play it, to each group. Those without instruments can play the storm sound with body percussion sounds used in the previous exercise. Repeat the activity to ensure that everyone gets a chance to play an instrument.

Listening

Play Beethoven's 'Pastoral symphony', on cassette 4, track 13/CD 2, track 33. The music depicts a storm which begins loudly and ends quietly.

Ask the children:
• What do you think the music is about?
Encourage them to identify a storm, thunder, wind or rain.

Performing the song 'Tshiyoyo'

Play 'Tshiyoyo' on cassette 4, track 3/CD 2, track 23. Ask the children to sing with the recording.

Try putting together accompaniments with which the children are already familiar: Play a drone on F throughout the song. Play ostinato (repeated) rhythm patterns on untuned percussion instruments. Play ostinato (repeated) melodic patterns on tuned percussion instruments.

Without playing the track, ask several children to play these accompanying patterns while the rest of the class sing 'Tshiyoyo'.

The following is a suggestion for structuring the accompaniment:

1 Begin by playing the drone on F four times, on chime bar/metallophone.
2 Add a repeated rhythm pattern (rhythmic ostinato): 'short, short, long, long', on untuned percussion instruments.
3 Add a melodic pattern (melodic ostinato): repeatedly play F, F, G, E, F.
4 Add the song – start quietly and gradually get louder up to line 3, then gradually get quieter.
5 Gradually take away the singing, melodic ostinato and rhythmic ostinato. (Use a prearranged signal, so the children know when to stop.) End the piece with F on chime bar/metallophone, played four times on its own. Here is a linear representation of what it might look like.

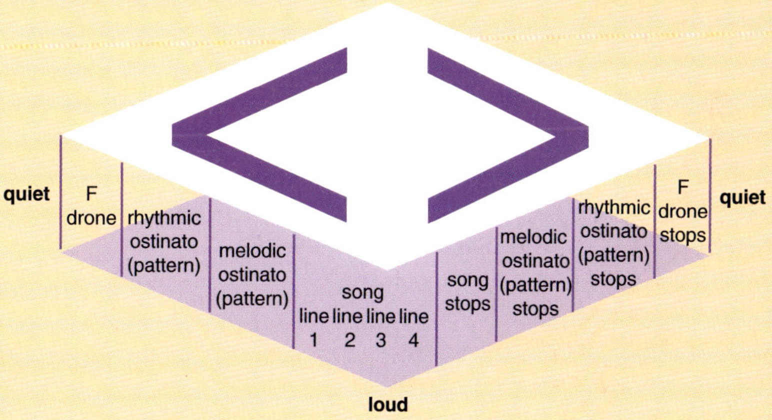

Tape record the children's performance and listen to it. Ask the children to decide if the performance got louder and then quieter.

Listening

Listen to an extract from the first movement of 'A sea symphony', by Vaughan Williams, on cassette 4, track 14/CD 2, track 34. The sounds in this extract start quietly, get gradually louder and then get quieter.

End-of-unit checkpoint:

Children should be able to show an understanding of the difference between loud and quiet sounds (dynamics): They should respond appropriately to symbols representing loud and quiet sounds. They should be able to control their loud and quiet sounds when performing together – both singing and playing instruments.

Unit 5: High and low sounds

Main Purpose

to understand that symbols can communicate levels of pitch

Main Skill

listening and recognising changes in levels of pitch and creating symbols to communicate levels of pitch

Musical Element

Main: Pitch

Other: Texture, Timbre, Dynamics, Structure

Main Stimuli

Songs: 'The old brass wagon'
'Hill an gully rida'

Main Activities

- musical games
- singing
- exploring sounds
- creating and reading from symbols
- responding to recorded music

Activity 1

Purpose:
to hear the difference between high and low sounds

Resources:
chime bars/metallophone, notes: C (high) and C (low)

Time guide:
5–10 minutes

Responding to high and low sounds

Play the two notes on chime bars/xylophone/metallophone. Ask the children to point to the ceiling when they hear the high sound and point to the floor when they hear the low sound. Gradually close the gap between the two notes, by playing notes closer together, so that the difference between high and low sounds is not so wide or obvious.

Activity 2

Purpose:
to recognise the difference between high sounds and low sounds from symbols; to perform high sounds and low sounds from symbols

Resources:
copymasters 20, 21, 22, 23, 24, two C chime bars (1 high and 1 low)

Time guide:
10–15 minutes

Playing high and low sounds in response to symbols

Display the flashcard, made from copymaster 20.

20

Ask the children:

- How do you think this would sound?

(One high sound followed by one low sound.)

Allow small groups of children to work with the flashcards.

21 22 23 24

They should perform the flashcards on chime bars, xylophone, or metallophone.

Extension: Without using flashcards, allow small groups of children to experiment with making high and low sounds. They should record their sounds, drawing symbols like those on the copymasters used in this activity.

Activity 3

Purpose:
to hear and recognise high, middle and low sounds, and to notate the sounds

Resources:
chime bars/xylophone/ metallophone, notes: C,E,G

Time guide
10–15 minutes

Working with pitched sounds

Draw on the board, or otherwise display, the following:

Play notes C, E and G in turn, to allow the children to hear the differences in pitch. Keep playing until the children are able to identify the high, middle and low sounds.

Ask one child to play a pattern on the three notes. Ask another child to record the sounds on the board (see the example over page).

Support point:
If you are using a xylophone/metallo-phone/glockenspiel, rather than the chime bars, then take all the bars which the children will not be using off the instrument.

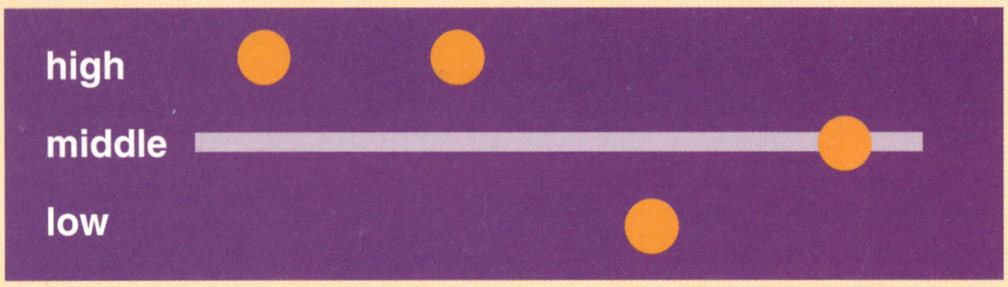

Extension: If you are able to sing and differentiate between pitched high, middle and low sounds confidently, sing the pattern the child has drawn.

Activity 4

Purpose:
to recognise pitch when singing

Resources:
cassette 5, track 2/CD 3, track 2

Time guide:
15 minutes

Singing and recording pitched sounds

Play the track and teach the children the song 'kite'.

Chorus: Floating way up high, way up in the sky,
Floating way back down, gently to the ground.
Lifted by the wind, darting up and down,
Colours pink and white and blue.

Verse: Kite in the sky, look at it fly,
Doing the Loop-de-loop and twirling round,
Kite in the sky, look at it fly,
Turning around and round.

Play the track again and ask the children to sing. This time, when the tune moves up or down in pitch, ask the children to draw a line in the air, contouring up and down where the music goes up or down. The contour of the tune is shown above the words.

Activity 5

Purpose:
to practise performing the pitch of sounds, getting higher and lower; combining pitched sounds with familiar rhythm patterns

Resources:
copymaster 3, xylophone/metallophone/chime bars, notes: C, D, E, G, A

Time guide:
10–15 minutes

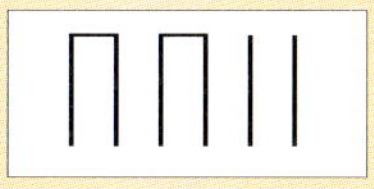

3

Support point:
If using a metallophone, remove F and B notes. The notes should be arranged to look like the diagram.

Combining rhythm patterns and pitched sounds

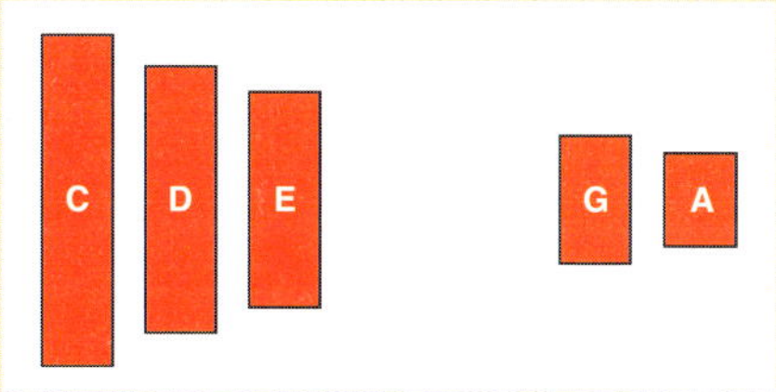

If you have enough tuned percussion instruments for three or four groups of children, divide the children accordingly.

Display the flashcard made from copymaster 3.

Ask the children to clap the rhythm on the card. Encourage them to say 'ta-tay, ta-tay, taa, taa' as they clap, to help them keep time. Count '1, 2, 3, 4', or use another prearranged signal, to ensure the children start clapping together.

Encourage the children to practise tapping the rhythm pattern lightly on their knees. (Later, they will play the same pattern on tuned percussion.)

Demonstrate playing the rhythm pattern on each of the 5 notes before allowing the children to try it out. Repeating the rhythm pattern on each of the five notes upwards and then downwards, as in the diagram below.

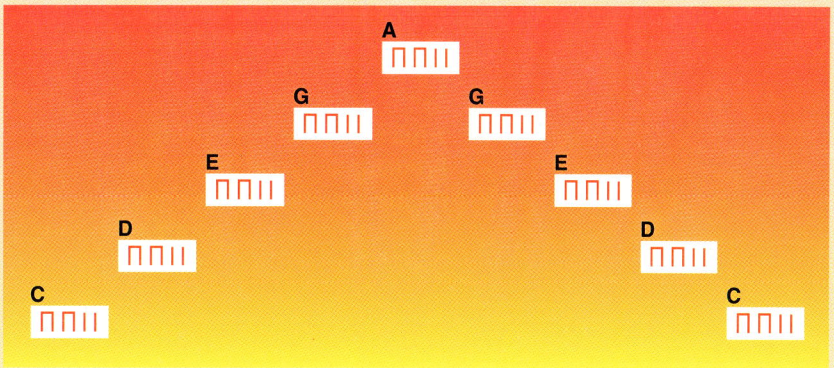

When the children are confident with this exercise, they can practise playing different rhythm patterns on the notes as they play e.g. play a flashcard on each note.

Section 1

Resources: cassette 5, track 3/CD 3, track 3, cassette 5, track 4/CD 3, track 4, xylophone/chime bars/ metallophone, notes: G, A, B, D

Time guide: 1 hour

Singing 'The old brass wagon'

Play 'The old brass wagon', on cassette 5, track 3/CD 3, track 3, and teach the children the song.

Circle to the left, the old brass wagon,
Circle to the left, the old brass wagon,
Circle to the left, the old brass wagon,
You're the one my darling.
Swing, oh swing, old brass wagon,
Swing, oh swing, old brass wagon,
Swing, oh swing, old brass wagon,
You're the one my darling.
Promenade home, old brass wagon,
Promenade home, old brass wagon,
Promenade home, old brass wagon,
You're the one my darling.

When the children are familiar with the tune, ask them:

- What happens to the music on the words 'Circle to the left' – do the sounds get higher, lower, or stay the same? (The sounds stay the same.)
- Each time 'Circle to the left' is repeated in the song,

something happens to the pitch – does it get higher or lower? (The pitch gets higher.)

Play the track again. If the children are not able to answer the question straight away, you can give them a clue by drawing a horizontal line in the air each time 'Circle to the left', is played. Draw the line higher each time. Ask the children to copy your actions.

Support point: When the children show the relative levels of pitch, with their hands, it should be clear whether their hands are moving up or down appropriately.

Circle to the left, the old brass wagon, circle to the left, the old brass wagon, circle to the left

Give out two or three tuned instruments. Ask one child to play G, A, B (the notes next to each other). Ask the children:
• What happens to the pitch – does it get higher or lower? (higher)

• Is each note a leap higher than the last, or only a step? (a step)

Explain that the notes, G, A, B, can be played with the song, 'The old brass wagon'.

Observation point: Identify those children who are able to answer questions about the relative pitch of sounds. Also, identify children who were able to play notes G, A, B in the correct place.

Play G on the first phrase of 'Circle to the left' (line 1). Play A on the second phrase of 'Circle to the left' (line 2). Play B on the third phrase of 'Circle to the left' (line 3). Play with the words of the phrase 'Circle to the left' only. The rest of the class should continue to sing with the track. Repeat the activity to allow different children the chance to play G, A, B.

Add a drone accompaniment on notes G and D. Play the notes simultaneously on the shaded words.

Perform the song with the track, adding the drone and the G, A, B pattern.

Creating sounds with pitch

If you have only one or two tuned instruments in your school, you will need to organise small groups of children to do this exercise, whilst the rest of the class is engaged in a different subject.

Give each group of children a tuned percussion instrument each to work with. Ask the children to create a pattern of sounds which includes the following: notes moving upwards step by step; notes moving downwards step by step; the same note played repeatedly.

The children should play their sound patterns on three notes only. The children can sequence their sound patterns

in different ways e.g. child one – B, A, G; child two – E, D, C; child 3 – F, F, F; child 4 – G, A, B; child 5 – G, G, G.

When the group has created their sequence of sound patterns, they should write down the letter names of the notes they have used, in the order they were played.

Let each child in the group try to perform this whole sequence alone. Encourage the other group members to try to help where necessary.

Observation point: Identify those groups who were able to understand and perform the task.

If the groups are working away from the whole class, tape record their outcomes and play them back for the whole class. If the whole class is working on the exercise simultaneously, the groups can come together and share their results when they are ready to do so. Encourage the class to recognise the different movements of notes getting higher, notes getting lower and the same note being repeated.

Listening

Listen to the extract from 'Trisch Trasch Polka', on cassette 5, track 4/CD 3, track 4. Ask the children to listen for some very obvious leaps moving upwards as well as some sequences that move both upwards and downwards by step. Ask the children:

• Are the beats groups in twos, threes, or fours?
(twos)

Section 2

Resources: cassette 5, track 3/CD 3, track 3, cassette 5, track 4/CD 3, track 4, paper/card, a range of tuned and untuned percussion instruments

Time guide: 1 hour

Creating symbols for pitched sound

Choose a xylophone, metallophone or glockenspiel and, concealing the instrument from the children, play the lowest and then the highest note.

Ask the children:

- Was there a step or a leap between the two notes, or did they stay the same?
(leap)

- Was the second note higher or lower?
(higher)

Encourage the children to suggest how they would draw a symbol to represent the sounds played in different ways. Ask the children to draw their suggestions on the board. Discuss as a whole class whether symbols are appropriate. If the children do not suggest any symbols, allow them to choose between the following:

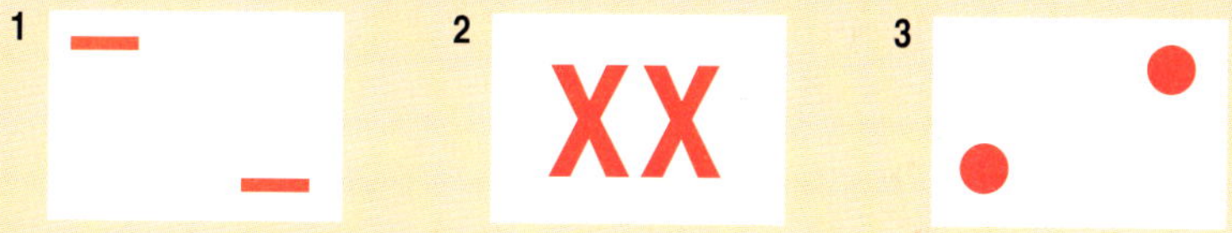

1 high to low leap

2 two notes staying the same

3 low to high leap

Divide the children into pairs and give each pair an instrument and some paper. Give out as many tuned instruments as you have. Encourage the pairs to play a simple pattern on their instrument and create a symbol for it.

Those children with tuned percussion instruments can create symbols for pitched sounds – notes getting higher/lower by step/leap, notes which stay the same.

Those children who have an untuned percussion instrument which is capable of producing two tones e.g. wooden agogo, can combine the way they play the different tones e.g. tap high sound, scrape low sound. They can create different symbols for these sounds.

Support point:
If, at any point, you need to talk to the children, use a prearranged signal to stop them performing and discussing e.g. raise your hand.

Those children who have untuned percussion instruments should try to play their instrument in different ways e.g. loudly/quietly, tap/scrape.

When the children are ready to do so, they can share their symbols with the rest of the class. Encourage the children to think about whether a person outside their group would be able to understand and perform from their symbol.

Observation point: Identify those children who are able to produce symbols which are easy for others to understand.

Although the symbols have been created for specific instruments, encourage the children to think about whether it would be possible for any other instrument to perform from the symbol. The children should discuss and explore these issues.

As a whole class, the children can choose those symbols which they feel to be most appropriate, and these can be made into flashcards.

Singing and performing from symbols

Sing 'Old brass wagon' with cassette 5, track 3/CD 3, track 3. Ask children to add the sound pattern on notes G, A, B and the drone on notes G and D, which they worked on in Section 1.

Ask the children to create symbols to show the G, A, B pattern: they should show each of the three notes repeated three times, getting higher each time they are played. Ask a volunteer to draw a suggested symbol on the board. Show the children flashcards made from copymasters 21, 22 and 25, as an example.

22 25 21

Display your symbols and perform the G, A, B accompaniment from them as the song is sung.

Listening

Play 'Trisch Trasch Polka' on cassette 5, track 4/CD 3, track 4. This time, allow the children to draw a line in the air to show the high and low sounds in the music. They will hear that the music begins with two upwards (higher) leaps, then a downwards (lower) run. The music then makes two upwards leaps, followed by an upwards run. The following diagram shows the upward leaps and downwards runs.

Support point: Encourage the children to listen carefully, so that their hand movements will fit the pitch of the music.

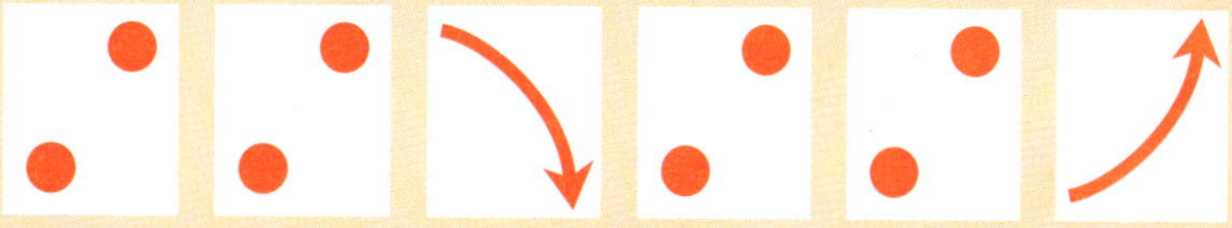

upwards leap | upwards leap | downwards run | upwards leap | upwards leap | upwards run

Dance for 'The old brass wagon'

Teach the children the following dance to 'The old brass wagon', on cassette 5, track 3/CD 3, track 3.

Ask the children to stand in a circle. (Their partner is the child on their right.)

Verse 1:
Hold hands and move to the left, in time to the steady beat of the music. On the last line of the verse, drop hands, link right arms with your partner and turn on the spot.

Verse 2:
Link arms with your partner and turn on the spot in time to the music.

Verse 3:
Hold hands with your partner. Pairs should walk in a circle, facing to the right. On the last line of the verse, link arms with your partner and turn on the spot.

Section 3

Resources: cassette 5, track 5/CD 3, track 5, cassette 5, track 6/CD 3, track 6, flashcards made in Section 2, xylophone/metallophone/chime bars, note: F, a selection of tuned and untuned percussion instruments

Time guide: 1 hour

Singing and recognising pitch

'Hill an gully rida' is a Jamaican call and response work song which was sung by men building new roads. It refers to the uneven countryside through which the new road had to be cut.

Play the children the song, on cassette 5, track 5/CD 3, track 5, and instruct them to listen to the song. Ask the children:

- What do you notice about the response lines – 'Hill an gully'?

Encourage them to identify that the tune is the same every time, and the notes are repeated. (The lines in italics are the response.)

Hill an gully rida,
Hill an gully.
Hill an gully rida,
Hill an gully.
An ah ben dung low dung,
Hill an gully.
An ah low dung bessy dung,
Hill an gully.
Hill an gully rida,
Hill an gully.
Hill an gully rida,
Hill an gully.
An yu better mind yu tumble dung,
Hill an gully.
An yu tumble dung yu bruk yu neck,
Hill an gully.

Play the track again and encourage the children to sing the response each time it occurs, and show the level of the pitch with their hands. When they have sung the song, ask for a volunteer to draw a line or a symbol, on the board, to show that the pitch is the same, e.g.

or

Play the track again and teach the children the rest of the song, explaining that 'bessy dung' means 'bend down'. Ask

the children:

- What do you notice about the pitch of 'Hill an gully rida' – is it the same, or different, each time it's sung? (The pitch stays the same.)

- Does the pitch of 'An ah ben dung low dung' and 'An ah low dung bessy dung' get higher or lower? (lower)

Play the track again and, this time, encourage one or two children to play percussion instruments on 'Hill an gully' each time it occurs in the song. Remind the children that the pitch is repeated. They should play on F. (It is worth reminding children that F is not the same as F#.) Repeat this a few times, so that other children have a chance to play. Encourage the rest of the class to clap the rhythm of 'Hill an gully', along with the tuned percussion. They should do this instead of singing the phrase. The song's 'response' will then be played and clapped.

Listening

Listen to the following extract, 'Canon', by Pachebel, on cassette 5, track 6/CD 3, track 6. Throughout the piece you can hear a repeated pitch pattern, played by the cellos, double bass and harpsichord.

> **Observation point:** Identify those children who play sounds which are appropriate to the symbols.

Performing pitched sound from flashcards

Display four of the flashcards that you made from the children's symbols in the last Section. Put out a selection of tuned and untuned percussion instruments and ask four children to choose the instruments to play the sounds represented on the symbols.

The following is an example of what you may have and the instruments that the children might choose to play these sounds.

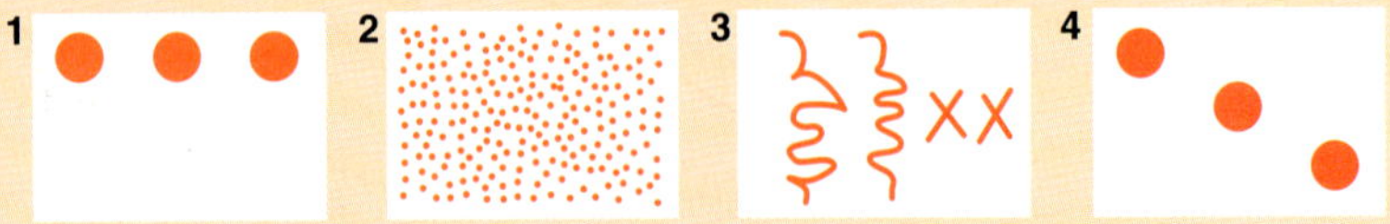

1 xylophone playing three high pitched notes.

2 shaking instrument

3 wooden agogo scraped twice and tapped twice.

4 xylophone playing three pitches (high, middle, low).

Experiment by sorting the flashcards in different ways: all pitched sound symbols together, in a row; all unpitched sound symbols together, in a row; a mixture of pitched and unpitched sound symbols together in a row.

Put two of the rows of flashcards together. Ask two children to play a row each. They should play at the same time.

Extension: Set the children the task of using the flashcards to create a piece of music. Let them work in groups and arrange the flashcards into an order that they choose. They should select instruments to play the flashcards and then perform from them.

Section 4

Resources: cassette 5, track 7/CD 3, track 7, flashcards made from children's symbols in Section 2, xylophone/metallophone/glockenspiel, notes: G, A, B, D, E, a selection of untuned percussion instruments

Time guide: 1 hour

Creating a rondo with pitched sounds

A rondo is a musical structure in which one part (A) keeps returning after new parts (B/C etc.) have been played e.g. ABACADA.

Remind the children of the rhythm pattern they clapped for 'Hill an gully'. Let them clap the rhythm of the words again, twice.

This rhythm, performed twice on untuned percussion instruments, is going to be part A of the rondo. Children without instruments can perform the A part with body percussion. Part B, C and D of the rondo will be played on tuned percussion instruments.

If you don't have many tuned percussion instruments, the same instrument may need to be played in different parts e.g. a xylophone may be played in part B by one child, in part C by another and in part D by yet another. You will need to ensure that children are confident about what to play and when. Restrict the notes used on the tuned percussion instruments to G, A, B, D, E. (Remove the F and C bars).

Support point:
Display the flashcards, so that each group playing can see their flashcards easily. Make sure the children can see you.

Part B:
Choose six flashcards. These should be a mixture of symbols showing pitch moving upwards (getting higher) step by step and moving downwards (getting lower) by leaps.

Decide which instruments should perform from these cards and in which order the flashcards are to be performed. This should be part B.

Part C:
Choose six different flashcards from the selection. These should be a mixture, showing pitch moving downwards (getting lower) step by step and upwards (getting higher) by leaps. Decide which instruments are going to play these flashcards, and in which order they should play them. This should be part C.

Part D:
Choose four more cards from the selection of flashcards. These should show the same pitched sound being repeated.

Choose tuned percussion instruments to play these cards and decide in which order they should be played. This should be part D.

Divide the class into four groups, and allow the children to perform their parts in a given order.

You can start the children off by clapping the 'Hill an gully' rhythm each time, for part A. Any children who are left without an instrument should be attached to the A group, and play the rhythm by clapping.

Performing the rondo

The rondo can be performed in the following way.

A Play the rhythm of 'Hill an gully'.

B Play a mixture of sounds moving upwards step by step and downwards by leaps. The following shows what your symbols might look like:

A Play the rhythm of 'Hill an gully'.

C Play a mixture of sounds moving downwards step by step and upwards by leaps.

A Play the rhythm of 'Hill an gully'.

D Play sounds at the same pitch.

A Play the rhythm of 'Hill an gully'.

Record the children's performance. Repeat this allowing different children to play the instruments. Choose different flashcards to represent the sounds. Record this new performance, and compare the two.

Extension:

1 If you have enough flashcards, display two rows of flashcards and ask two groups of children to play a row each at the same time, so that some texture is created.

2 One way of involving more children with the musical sections involving pitched sounds is to allow those who are confident to do so to use their voices. They should sing the same notes as the tuned percussion instruments. Also, if there are several children in your class learning instruments such as recorders, flutes or violins, they can play the notes on their instruments.

Listening

Play the rondo, from Mozart's 4th horn concerto, on cassette 5, track 7/CD 3, track 7. Ask the children to listen for the A part which reappears many times.

End-of-unit checkpoint:

Children should be able to: create symbols to show that sounds are repeated, or that they move up (higher)/down (lower) in a step or a leap; perform from symbols representing changes in pitch; listen to and recognise changes in the pitch of sounds.

Unit 6: Sounds and musical shapes

Main Purpose

to provide opportunities to experience music from different traditions

Main Skill

to listen, respond and appraise music from other cultures and traditions

Musical Element

Main: Structure, Tempo

Other: Duration, Pitch, Dynamics, Timbre

Main Stimuli

British, African, Eastern European, middle Eastern and Indian music

Main Activities:

- singing
- exploring sounds
- creating effects
- dancing with songs
- responding to recorded music

This unit focuses on music from different countries and traditions. It involves the children in thinking about what makes the music sound different. The skills which are developed in this unit cover several elements and help to develop children's listening skills.

Activity 1

Purpose:
to recognise when music gets faster and slower and respond by using body percussion to keep the steady beat

Resources:
cassette 5, track 8/CD 3, track 8

Time guide:
5–10 minutes

Listening and keeping the steady beat

Play the children 'Beat feat' on cassette 5, track 8/CD 3, track 8. Ask the children to keep the steady beat by clapping. Ask the children:

- Does the steady beat stay at the same speed throughout?

Encourage the children to identify that it gets faster and then slows down again.

When the children are confident about keeping the steady beat all the way through the music, allow one child to lead the activity with their chosen type of body percussion.

Activity 2

Purpose:
to respond, through movement, to changes of tempo in the music

Resources:
cassette 5, track 9/CD 3, track 9

Time guide:
5–10 minutes

Where:
the hall

Moving to fast and slow music

Play 'Changes', on the cassette/CD and ask the children to walk around the hall, keeping in step to the steady beat. They should get faster and slower where appropriate. Encourage the children to walk faster, rather than run, when the beat becomes faster.

Encourage the children to show changes in speed in ways other than walking, e.g. move higher/lower; move in different directions - leaping, turning, jumping and rolling.

Encourage the children to work in pairs and create a sequence of movement. One child should move to the fast tempo of the music and the other to the slow tempo. Encourage them to find ways of moving from fast to slow and vice versa.

Activity 3

Purpose:
to perform a chant with control, keeping the steady beat as the tempo gets faster/slower

Resources:
cassette 5, track 10/CD 3, track 10, cassette 5, track 11/CD 3, track 11, cassette 5, track 12/CD 3, track 12

Time guide:
10–15 minutes

Performing a fast and slow chant

Play the children version 1 of 'Boom-chick-a-boom' on the cassette 5, track 10/CD 3, track 10. Teach them the rhyme and encourage them to say the rhyme rhythmically, performing only the echo.

Leader:	Say 'Boom chick-a-boom'
Echo:	Say 'Boom chick-a-boom'
Leader:	Say 'Boom chick-a-boom'
Echo:	Say 'Boom chick-a-boom'
Leader:	Say 'Boom chick-a-rock-a, Chick-a-rock-a, Chick-a-boom'
Echo:	Say 'Boom chick-a-rock-a, Chick-a-rock-a, Chick-a-boom'
Leader:	'Ah-ha!'
Echo:	'Ah-ha'
Leader:	'Eh-hee!'
Echo:	'Ee-hee!'
Leader:	'One more time'
Echo:	'One more time'
Leader:	'Faster'
Echo:	'Faster'

Play version 2 of 'Boom-chick-a-boom' on cassette 5, track 11/CD 3, track 11. Encourage the children to clap the steady beat on the echo, as they say the rhyme. The steady beat is indicated by the shaded words.

This version of the rhyme has more than one verse, and the verses get faster. Make sure that the children keep the beat steady as the chant gets faster.

Play version 3, on cassette 5, track 12/CD 3, track 12 and encourage the children to say the rhyme and clap the steady beat again on the echo. This time the steady beat gets slower.

Activity 4

Purpose:
to create rhythm sequences from patterns of words

Resources:
tambour, wood-block, finger castanets, pop jingle (tapped on edge), cowbell, wooden agogo

Time guide:
15–20 minutes

Performing the rhythm of words

Encourage the children to think of their favourite food and ask them to practise clapping the rhythm of the words e.g. 'fish and chips' (3 claps), 'sausages and chips' (5 claps).

Encourage the children to clap the words as they would say them – using the same rhythm, speed and emphasis. When they are confident to play their rhythm, divide the children into pairs. Let one child clap the pattern of their favourite food. They should keep repeating this. The second child should add the steady beat.

When the pair are able to perform these two patterns together, let one try playing the rhythm pattern and the other its steady beat, on untuned percussion instruments. Encourage the children to think about how they are going to start and stop their sequence.

Extension: If you have any pairs who are finding the task very easy, let them join another pair who are also finding the task easy. Together, they can perform the rhythm for three 'food' words, one after another. (They should decide on the order in which to clap the words.) The fourth child should try to play the steady beat of this rhythm.

Activity 5

Purpose:
listen to music, recognise and talk about the difference between melody and rhythm

Resources:
cassette 5, track 13/CD 3, track 13, cassette 5, track 14/CD 3, track 14

Time guide:
10 minutes

Rhythm and melody

Explain to the children that you will play them two extracts. On the first extract the melody (tune) is the most noticeable feature and on the second, rhythm is the most noticeable feature. Ask the children to listen to the extracts, and decide which shows rhythm and which shows melody. Ask the children:

- Can you tell me which instrument(s) were playing the melody?
  (flute)
- Can you tell me which instruments were playing the rhythm?
  (drums)

The first extract on cassette 5, track 13/CD 3, track 13 is called 'Syrinx', by Debussy. It was written for an unaccompanied flute. The second extract on cassette 5, track 14/CD 3, track 14 is 'Hiryu Sand An Gaeshi', played by a Japanese drum ensemble.

Activity 6

Purpose:
to recognise and talk about changes to melody

Resources:
cassette 5, track 15/CD 3, track 15, cassette 5, track 16/CD 3, track 16, cassette 5, track 17/CD 3, track 17, cassette 5, track 18/CD 3, track 18

Time guide:
5–10 minutes

Changing melody

The first two extracts on cassette 5, track 15/CD 3, track 15 and cassette 5, track 16/CD 3, track 16, are taken from the last movement of the 'Violin concerto' by Katchachurian.

The second two extracts, the first on cassette 5, track 17/CD 3, track 17 and the second on cassette 5, track 18/CD 3, track 18, are taken from 'Greensleeves to a ground'. This is played on the treble recorder. Ask the children the following questions, which can apply to both sets of extracts:

- Is the melody (tune) the same both times?

(no)

- How is the music different in the second piece?

In each second extract, more notes (trills and decoration) have been added.

Section 1

Resources: cassette 5, track 19/CD 3, track 19, cassette 5, track 20/CD 3, track 20, cassette 5, track 21/CD 3, track 21, cassette 5, track 22/CD 3, track 22, cassette 5, track 23/CD 3, track 23, a tape recorder, a selection of tuned and untuned percussion instruments

Time guide: 1 hour

This Section focuses on some examples of British music. If the school's local area has any musical tradition associated with it, this can provide a useful resource, and will tie in with children's studies of the local area in Geography.

Collecting sounds from local areas

Tape record different sounds which are produced in the local area: trade and industry, shops, churches, parks, farms, traffic, train stations etc. Identify, and make a note for yourself, of the sounds in the order in which you tape them.

Play the sounds to the children. If you have a map of the local area, point to the places where you recorded the sounds, as you hear them.

Finding matching sounds

Encourage the children to try to recreate some of the environmental sounds which they heard on the recording. They should use percussion instruments, vocal sounds and body percussion, to try to make similar sounds.

Play the tape recording again, and discuss with the children what types of instruments e.g. wooden/metal sounds, or ways of playing, e.g. shaking/scraping, will be needed to reproduce each sound heard. Ask the children to think about the following questions, when creating their sounds.

- Does the sound have a rhythm?
- Can you hear one sound/many sounds?
- Is the sound loud/quiet?
- Is the sound high/low?
- Is the sound short/long?

If the children are creating sounds to represent environmental sounds heard in a park, they should think about the following questions:

- Is it raining in the park? How can we make rain sounds?

Encourage the children to identify shaking instruments, and tapping drums with fingers.

- Is it windy in the park? How can we make sounds for the wind?
Encourage the children to identify voices, rubbing drum skins and shaking instruments.

Observation point: Identify those children who are able to find appropriate sound sources to recreate the environmental sounds. Also, identify those children who join in the discussion and have developed some musical vocabulary with which to express their views about the sounds heard.

- Was the park empty? How can we use sounds to convey that?
Encourage the children to identify instruments which are capable of producing sustaining sounds e.g. cymbal, indian bells, a drone or a slow ostinato (repeated) rhythm pattern played on a metallophone.

- Was the park full? How can we make the busy sounds we heard?
The children can use their voices to reproduce the sounds of e.g. dogs barking, ducks quacking, children playing.

Allow the children to work in groups. Each group should be allocated a different location where recordings were made. The group should discuss and choose appropriate sounds.

When the children are ready, ask them to share with the rest of the class the sounds they have created as a group. Ask the whole class to think about and discuss whether the sounds chosen effectively conveyed environmental sounds (or silence) and their atmosphere.

Performing a sound piece

A map can be used as a graphic score. Mark the locations where the environmental sounds were recorded. Allow the class to decide in which order they will, musically, visit those locations. Point to each location and the group who have been working on those sounds should produce their sounds until you point to another location. This will help to give the sound piece structure, and allows the children some direction in knowing when to stop and start performing.

Tape record the children's performance. Play the sounds back for the children to listen, and point to the appropriate location on the map as the sounds are made.

Listening

In 'The lark ascending', by Vaughan Williams, on cassette 5, track 19/CD 3, track 19, the violin gives the impression of the lark's song and flight in the English countryside.

The second extract, on cassette 5, track 20/CD 3, track 20, is called 'Knightsbridge march', by Eric Coates. On this recording it is performed by a brass band. There is a long tradition of brass band playing in different areas of Britain.

Singing 'The riddle song'

Play version 1 of 'The riddle song', an English folk song, on cassette 5, track 21/CD 3, track 21. Teach the children the song.

I gave my love a cherry that has no stones.
I gave my love a chicken that has no bones.
I gave my love a ring that has no end.
I gave my love a baby that's no cryen'.

How can there be a cherry that has no stones?
How can there be a chicken that has no bones?
How can there be a ring that has no end?
How can there be a baby that's no cryen'?

A cherry when it's blooming, it has no stones.
A chicken when it's piping, it has no bones.
A ring when it's rolling, it has no end.
A baby when it's sleeping, there's no cryen'.

When the children are familiar with the song, talk about the words, to see if the children have understood them.

Explain to the children that the song was collected by Cecil Sharp in the early 19th century. Cecil Sharp collected and wrote down most of the old English folk songs which had previously belonged only to an oral tradition. Most of the old English folk songs which have survived were written down by Cecil Sharp. He found this song in the southern Appalacian mountains, North America, where most of the inhabitants were of English descent. The song, like most of those he collected, was traditionally sung without accompaniment.

Play the children version 2 of the song on cassette 5, track 22/CD 3, track 22. Ask them to listen to this unaccompanied version of the song. Play the children version 3 on cassette 5, track 23/CD 3, track 23. You will hear the song played with accompaniment. Ask the children to state a preference.

Extension: Ask the children to write some riddles of their own.

Section 2

Resources: cassette 5, track 24/CD 3, track 24, cassette 5, track 25/CD 3, track 25, cassette 6, track 2/CD 3, track 26, cassette 6, track 3/CD 3, track 27, cassette 6, track 4/CD 3, track 28, *untuned percussion instruments:* drums, tambour; *tuned percussion instruments:* chime bars/xylophone/ metallophone, notes: D, A, C#, B, A

Time guide: 1 hour

This Section introduces children to both popular African music, and traditional music from certain rural areas. In Africa, as all over the world, music is integrated into the rituals and concerns of other areas of social life and there are, of course, many and varied musical traditions within the continent.

Singing 'Everybody loves saturday night'

This song comes from Ghana.

Play version 1 of the song on cassette 5, track 24/CD 3, track 24. The steady beat (indicated by the shaded words and blocks) can be heard clearly on this version. Ask the children to keep the beat by patting their knees.

1 Ev'ry body loves saturday night.
2 Ev'ry body loves saturday night.
3 Ev'rybody, ev'rybody, ev'rybody, ev'rybody
4 Ev'rybody loves saturday night.

Play the track again and ask the children to sing the song. Give a drum/tambour to two children and ask them to play the steady beat whilst the rest of the class sing the song.

Encourage the children singing to clap the rhythm of the word 'Ev'rybody', in the third line of the song.

Play version 2 of the song on cassette 5, track 25/CD 3, track 25. Without singing, clap the rhythm with the clapping on the recording. (You will hear clapping at the end of lines 1, 2 and 4 and throughout line 3.)

When the children are confident to do so, they can perform the song adding the steady beat and clapping.

Extension: Add a drone on A and (lower) D: The notes should be played simultaneously on the steady beat.

If you have chromatic instruments, e.g. keyboards, you can ask the children to perform the following pattern of sounds on line 3:

D,	D,	D,	D,	(lower)	C#,	C#,	C#,	C#
(Ev' -	ry -	bod -	y)		(Ev' -	ry -	bod -	y)
B,	B,	B,	B		A,	A,	A,	A
(Ev' -	ry -	bod -	y)		(Ev' -	ry -	bod -	y)

Listening

Play the children the extract from 'Dagbamba drummers: Tora' on cassette 6, track 2/CD 3, track 26.

The Dagbamba people live about four hundred miles north of the coast in West Africa (northern Ghana). The drummers play together (there may be as many as fifty to a hundred) and accompany songs about the history of their former leaders. They attribute names to these leaders. These are called 'praise names' and become the basis of rhythm patterns for dance beats. Drummers will show respect for their neighbours by beating the rhythm of these names at social gatherings.

Talking drum

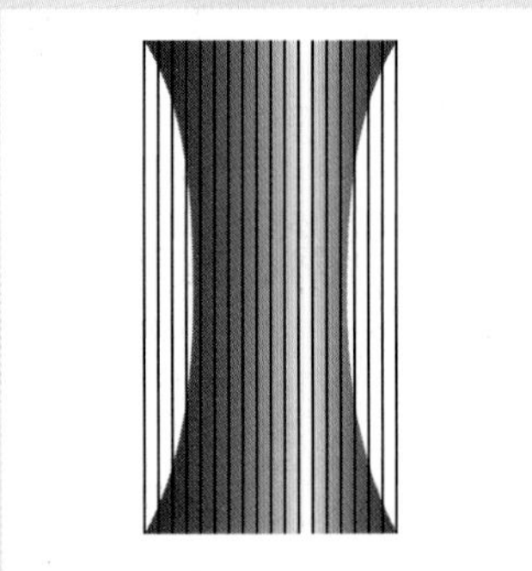

The Dagbamba drummers use three types of drums: a lunga, a gungon and a 'talking drum'.

The pitch on the 'talking drum' can be changed as the player squeezes the sides of the drum to tighten the head and hits the skin with a beater.

Observation point: Identify those children who are able to perform the rhythm patterns with the others in the group.

Extension: Encourage the children to think of 'praise names'. They can use the names of people they know or create special names. Ask them to practise clapping the rhythms of the names they choose. When the children can clap the rhythms confidently, they can try playing them on drums.

Divide the children into groups. Encourage the children to make up a short rhythm piece: they should play the rhythms of their praise names and add an accompanying steady beat.

Listening

Play 'Independence song', on cassette 6, track 3/CD 3, track 27. This is a traditional song from Tanzania. The following instruments can be heard: mbira (hand/thumb piano), zeze (small fiddle made from a gourd and hide).

Play 'Izithembifo Zenkozi', by Ladysmith Black Mambazo, a popular vocal group, on cassette 6, track 4/CD 3, track 28. Ask the children to listen to the different sounds made by performer's voices.

Encourage the children to talk about the differences between the two pieces.

Ask them to identify the same features of the two pieces of music they have heard e.g. strong rhythmic feel, African instruments.

Responding to music

After children have listened to music from the different cultures in each of the Sections of this unit, ask them to draw/paint, or write a poem in response to each piece, reflecting what the music suggests to them. Allow this activity to be quite open-ended to enable the children to express a free, creative response.

Section 3

Resources: cassette 6, track 5/CD 3, track 29, cassette 6, track 6/CD 3, track 30, cassette 6, track 7/CD 3, track 31, cassette 6, track 8/CD 3, track 32, cassette 6, track 9/CD 3, track 33, cassette 6, track 10/CD 3, track 34, cassette 6, track 11/CD 3, track 35, cassette 6, track 12/CD 3, track 36, tambourine, xylophone/metallophone, chime bars, notes: D and A

Time guide: 1 hour

Where: the hall

This section introduces the children to music from middle eastern and eastern European traditions.

Listening

Listen to an extract from a Hungarian piece called 'Dance from Maramaros' on cassette 6, track 5/CD 3, track 29. The instrument which helps to give the music its distinctive sound is the cimbalom. The children will hear the music get gradually faster until the end of the piece. 'Hava Nagilah', an Israeli song on cassette 6, track 6/CD 3, track 30, also gets gradually faster.

Singing 'Dayenu'

Play the children 'Dayenu', on cassette 6, track 7/CD 3, track 31, a Hebrew song for Pesach (Passover). Ask the children to listen to the song and keep the steady beat by clapping. The steady beat has been indicated by the shaded words.

1 He has led us out of Egypt, led His people out of Egypt,
He has led us out of Egypt, da-ye-nu.

Refrain: Da-da-ye-nu, da-da-ye-nu.
Da-da-ye-nu, da-ye-nu-da-ye-nu-da-ye-nu.
Da-da-ye-nu, da-da-ye-nu,
Da-da-ye-nu-da-ye-nu-da-ye-nu.

2 He has given us the Sabbath, given us the Holy Sabbath,
He has given us the Sabbath, da-ye-nu.

3 He has given us the Torah, given us the blessed Torah,
He has given us the Torah, da-ye-nu.

Ask the children:
• Did the steady beat stay the same speed throughout the song?
(The steady beat increased in speed.)

• Can you tell me whereabouts in the song the beat got faster?
Encourage the children to identify that the beat gets faster in the refrain.

Play the track again and teach the children the song. Ask half of the children to clap the steady beat as the rest of the class sing. Rotate this, so that all of the children get a chance to clap the steady beat. Play the track again and, this time, ask a few children to keep the steady beat on the tambourine, as the rest of the class sing along with the track.

Dancing to 'Dayenu'

In Middle Eastern countries, group dances are quite common. The dances are often done in a line or semi-circle. In Israel, such dances are called 'hora', in some Arab countries they are called 'debkee'.

Observation point: Identify those children who are able to step and hop, keeping time with the steady beat.

The 'hora' which accompanies 'Dayenu' is made up of simple steps:

1 Step with your right foot.

2 Hop with your right foot.

3 Step with your left foot.

4 Hop with your left foot.

When the children have practised these steps, ask them to get into lines of six or eight. They should always hold hands and face and move towards the right. They should try to step/hop on the steady beat of the song.

Start the lines of children in different places around the room and encourage them to listen carefully to the track as they respond by performing the dance.

Listening

Middle Eastern music often has many trills and musical decorations added. Ask the children to listen to the following extracts and try to identify some of the differences between the two versions of them. (In each case, the first version is the melody without any trills or musical decorations, the second version has these sounds added.)

Listen to the Hungarian piece 'Lamenting song', versions 1 and 2, played on the violin, on cassette 6, track 8/CD 3, track 32 and cassette 6, track 9/CD 3, track 33. Listen to the Bosnian song 'Is it clear or cloudy?' versions 1 and 2 on cassette 6, track 10/CD 3, track 34 and cassette 6, track 11/CD 3, track 35.

Singing 'Hey ho, hey lo'

Play the Slovakian song 'Hey ho, hey lo' on cassette 6, track 12/CD 3, track 36. Ask the children to clap the steady beat (indicated by the shaded words). Instruct the children to listen carefully and clap the steady beat faster as the tempo of the song changes.

Hey ho, hey lo, tambourines are ringing,
Hey ho, hey lo, ringing all a-round.
Listen, listen, hear them jingle, jangle,
Making music with a happy sound.
Faster, faster, how they jingle, jangle.
Making music with a happy sound.

Play the track again and teach the children the song. Allow some children to keep the steady beat, by tapping a tambourine, as the rest of the class sing the song.

Choose different children to play a drone on A and (lower) D: They should play the notes simultaneously on the steady beat.

Section 4

Resources: cassette 6, track 13/CD 3, track 37, cassette 6, track 14/CD 3, track 38, cassette 6, track 15/CD 3, track 39, cassette 6, track 16/CD 3, track 40, cassette 6, track 17/CD 3, track 41, drums, indian bells, jingle bells, cymbals chime bars/metallophone/xylophone, notes: B, D, E, G, A, B and C, Db, E, F#, A, C

Time guide: 1 hour

This Section introduces the children to Indian music.

Singing 'The lemon tree'

Play the children 'The lemon tree', on cassette 6, track 13/CD 3, track 37. This is a traditional Bengali wedding song. Teach the children the song.

Chorus:
Under the lemon tree, the happy bridegroom dresses himself.
Don't pick the lemons, my dear.
(sing twice)

1 I will go into the sta-ble
And pick out the best of all.
Pick out a horse whose teeth are healthy, for my wife.
Don't pick the lemons, my dear.

Chorus

2 I will go into the elephant house,
And pick out the best of all.
Pick out an elephant that's strong and mighty, for my wife.
Don't pick the lemons, my dear.

Chorus

3 I will go into the hen house,
And pick out the best of all.
Pick out a hen whose eggs are
tasty, for my wife.
Don't pick the lemons, my dear.

Play the track again and ask the children to clap the steady beat (as indicated), without singing.

Play the track again and, this time, ask half the class to sing the song and the other half to clap the steady beat without singing.

Choose two or three children and ask them to play a drone in accompaniment: They should play notes A and (lower) D together on the steady beat. Sing the song again, with the drone added.

Support point: Ensure that the children playing indian bells are also singing. This way, they will not be late in playing their sound.

Encourage the children to clap the rhythm of the words 'Don't pick the lemons my dear'. When the children are able to do this confidently, give out some jingle bells to a few children. Ask them to play the rhythm of the words 'Don't pick the lemons, my dear', at the end of each verse of the song.

Give indian bells to two children and ask them to play one sound every time they sing the word 'lemon(s)'.

Play the track and sing the song again. Add all of the accompaniments: the drone on notes A and (lower D); the jingle bells playing the rhythm pattern at the end of each verse; the indian bells playing on the word 'lemon(s)'.

Listening

The main instruments which are used in India, and which give certain Indian music its distinctive sound, are the sitar and the tablar.

The sitar is a stringed instrument which is played like a guitar. The strings on the sitar can be stretched so that the pitch of the note being played moves up and down very slightly.

The tablar is a pair of drums. These are played with the fingertips, cupped palms, the ball of the thumb, and other parts of the hand. This creates a range of different sounds, including light, heavy, sustaining and ringing.

Play the children a short extract of sitar music, on cassette 6, track 14/CD 3, track 38. Ask them to listen to the changing pitch of the sitar's sounds. Play the children a short extract of tablar music, on cassette 6, track 15/CD 3, track 39.

Indian music is very complex in the way in which it is put together. Melodies are based on 'raga' which are scales (patterns of notes). There is a specific 'rag' for each time of the day: early morning, mid-morning, early afternoon, early evening. There is also a specific 'rag' for the seasons, events and festivals.

Listening

Play the children the following extracts: The first, on cassette 6, track 16/CD 3, track 40, is a classical piece called 'Raga

Bairagi Todi', taken from the faster section of the whole piece, where the tablar join in with the sitar. The second extract, on cassette 6, track 17/CD 3, track 41, is Indian popular music. It is a Bhangra piece called 'Soniaye ni soniaye'.

Ask the children:
• Which piece did you prefer – the popular music, classical music or folk music?

• Can you describe some ways in which Indian music is different from British music?
Encourage them to identify e.g. that Indian music uses different instruments.

Creating a raga sound piece

Divide the children into small groups. Ask them to create their own sound patterns, using the following notes on tuned percussion instruments: C, Db, E, F#, A, C. They should add a drone to this on notes A and (lower) C. this is called a 'Rag vibha' – music for early morning/twilight.

Ask the children to play a piece based on a 'Rag malakosh' – music for the night: They should play a sound pattern on B, D, E, G, A, B and a drone on E and (lower) B.

They can add drums, tambours, indian bells and cymbals to the music.

Support point:
Db is the same note as C# .

With either of the raga, the children can play their sound pattern on as many or as few of the notes as they wish.

Children can think of words associated with morning or night (as appropriate) and play the rhythm of those words.

Extension: Select listening extracts from within this unit. Play them to the children and ask them to identify the music's country of origin. Ask them to explain, in their own words, how they were able to recognise them e.g. by identifying the instruments played.

End-of-unit checkpoint:

Children should be able to listen and respond to music from different musical traditions, recognise instruments and timbres specific to certain musical traditions, and create music in response to the music they have heard.

Taa, taa, taa, taa
(long, long, long, long)

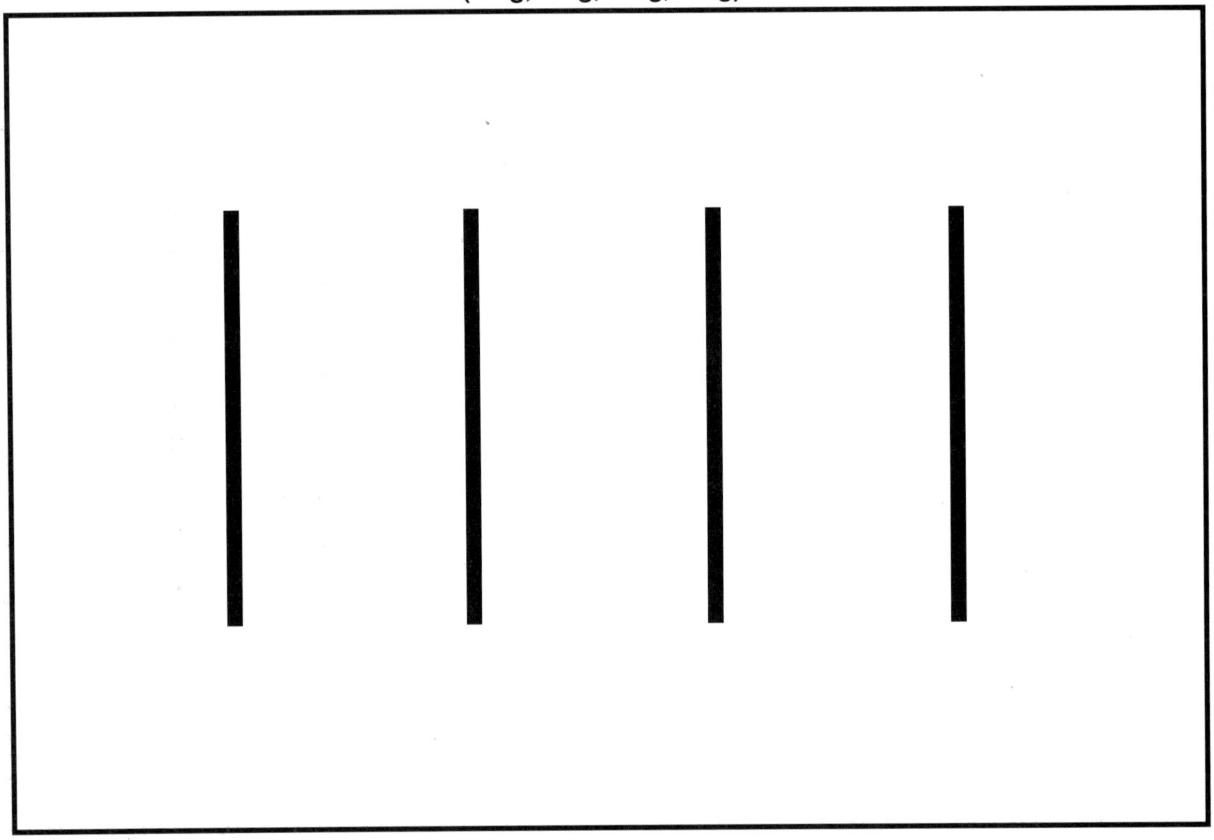

Taa, ta-tay, ta-tay, taa
(long, short-short, short-short, long)

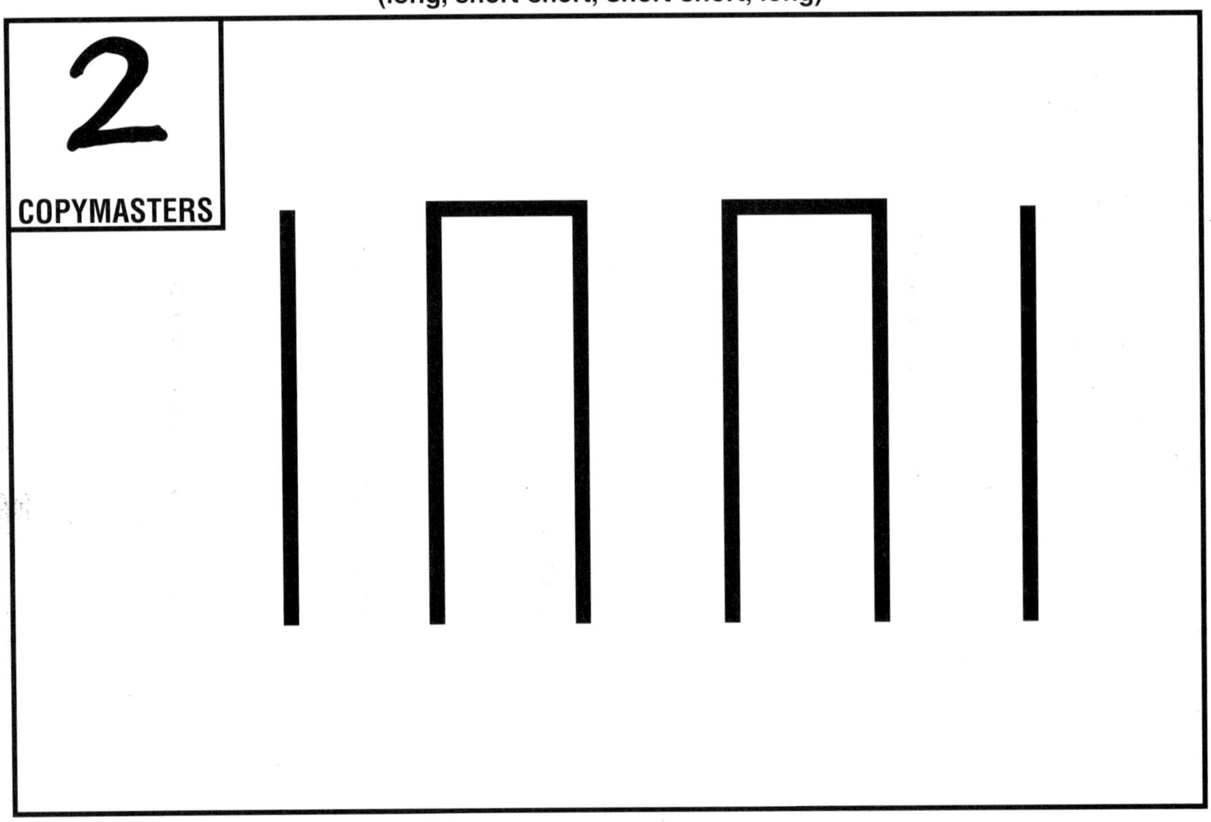

3

Ta-tay, ta-tay, taa, taa
(short-short, short-short, long, long)

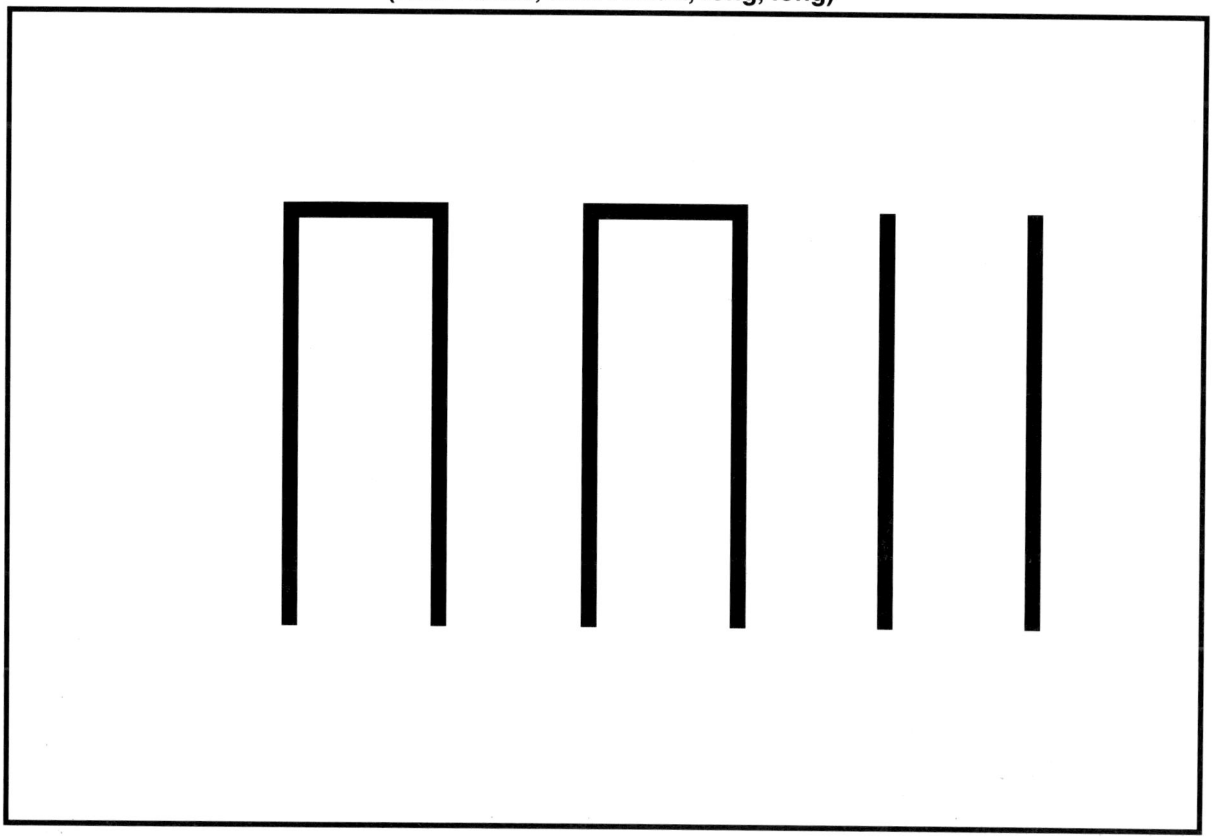

Taa, ta-tay, taa, taa
(long, short-short, long, long)

4

COPYMASTERS

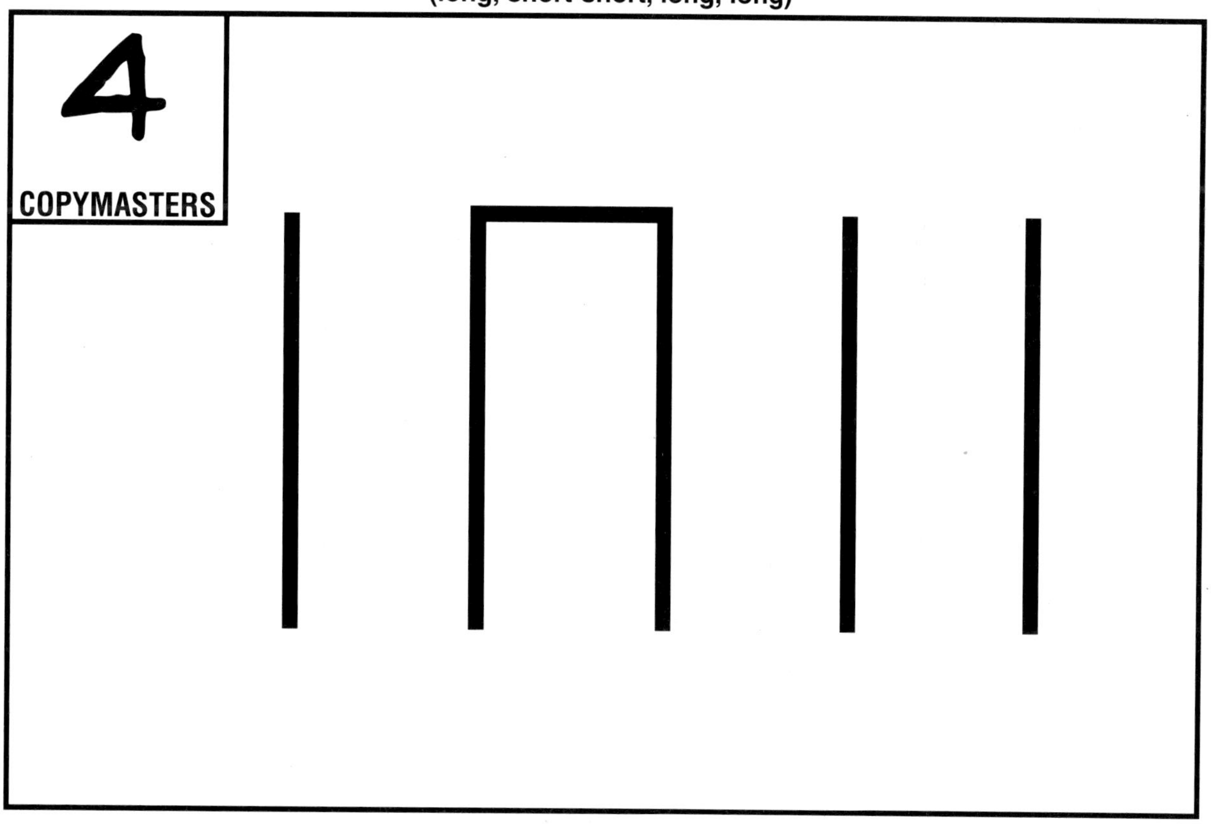

5

Taa, taa, taa
(long, long, long)

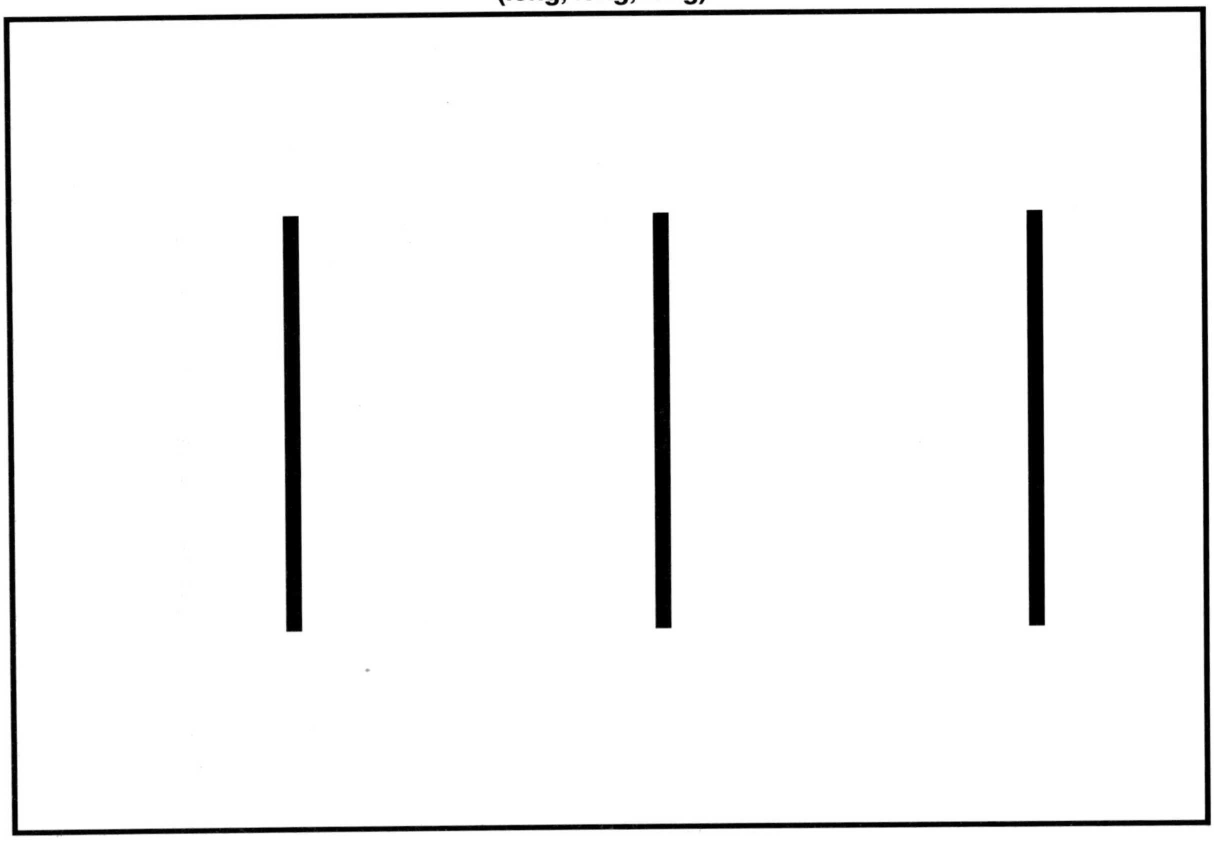

Taa, ta-tay, taa
(long, short-short, long)

6
COPYMASTERS

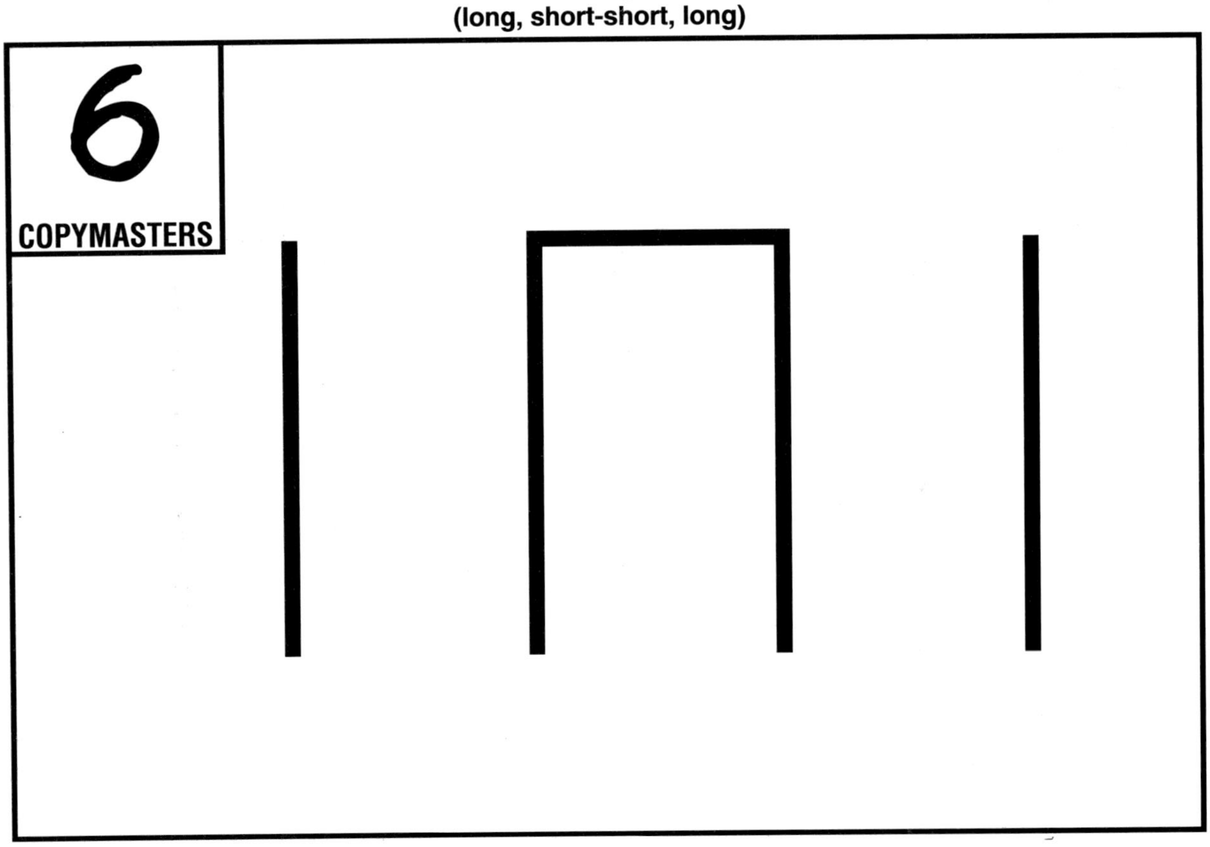

7

Taa, saa, taa
(long, rest, long)

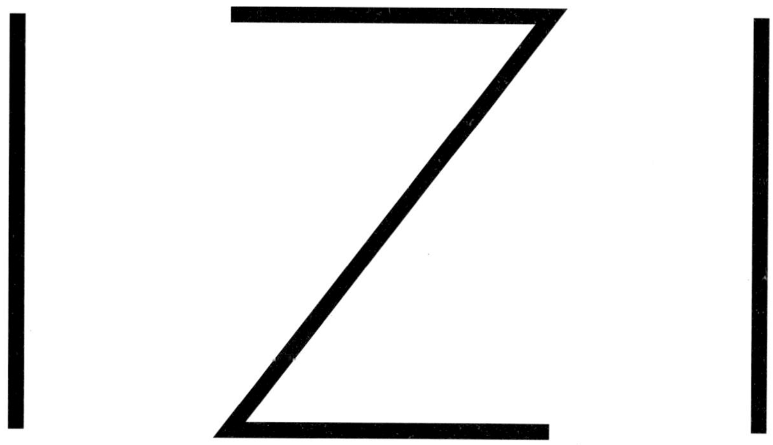

Taa, ta-tay, taa, ta-tay
(long, short-short, long, short-short)

8

COPYMASTERS

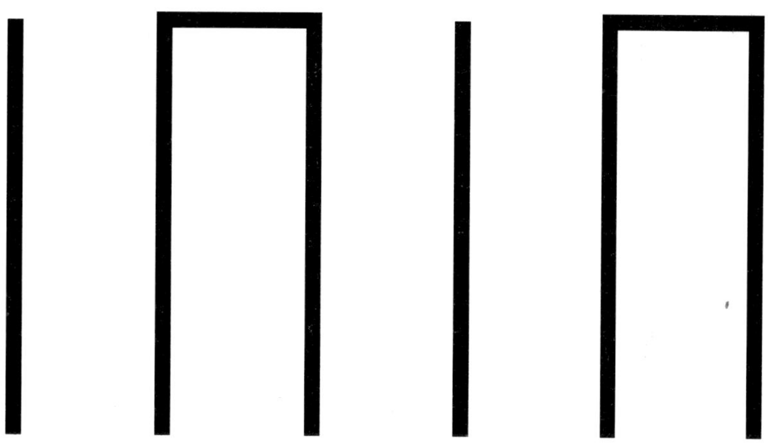

Taa, saa, taa, saa
(long, rest, long, rest)

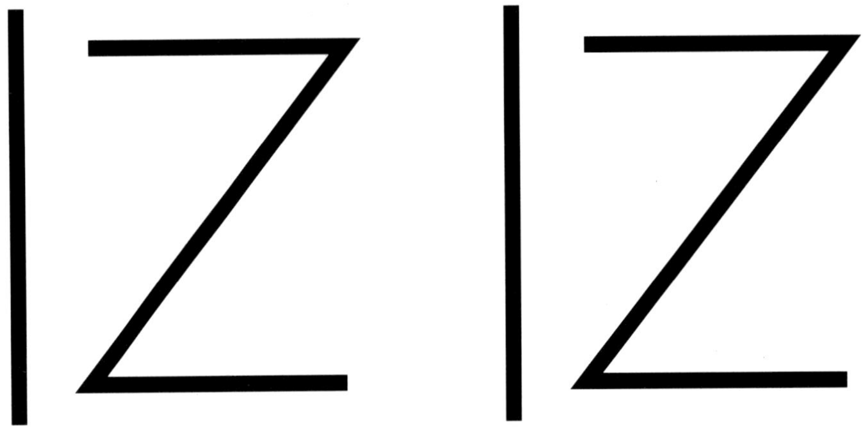

Quiet sound

10

COPYMASTERS

11

Taa, taa
(long, long)

Loud, loud

12

COPYMASTERS

13

Quiet, quiet

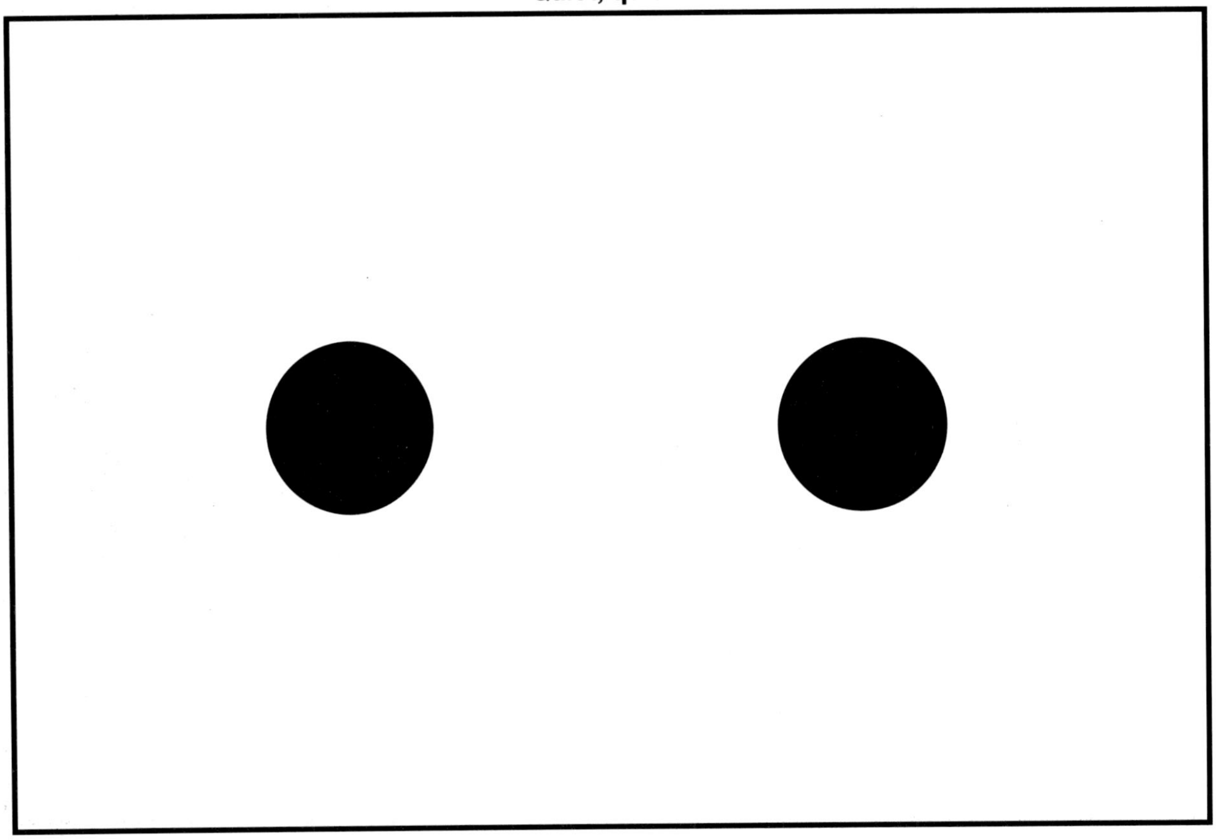

Loud, quiet, loud, quiet, loud

14
COPYMASTERS

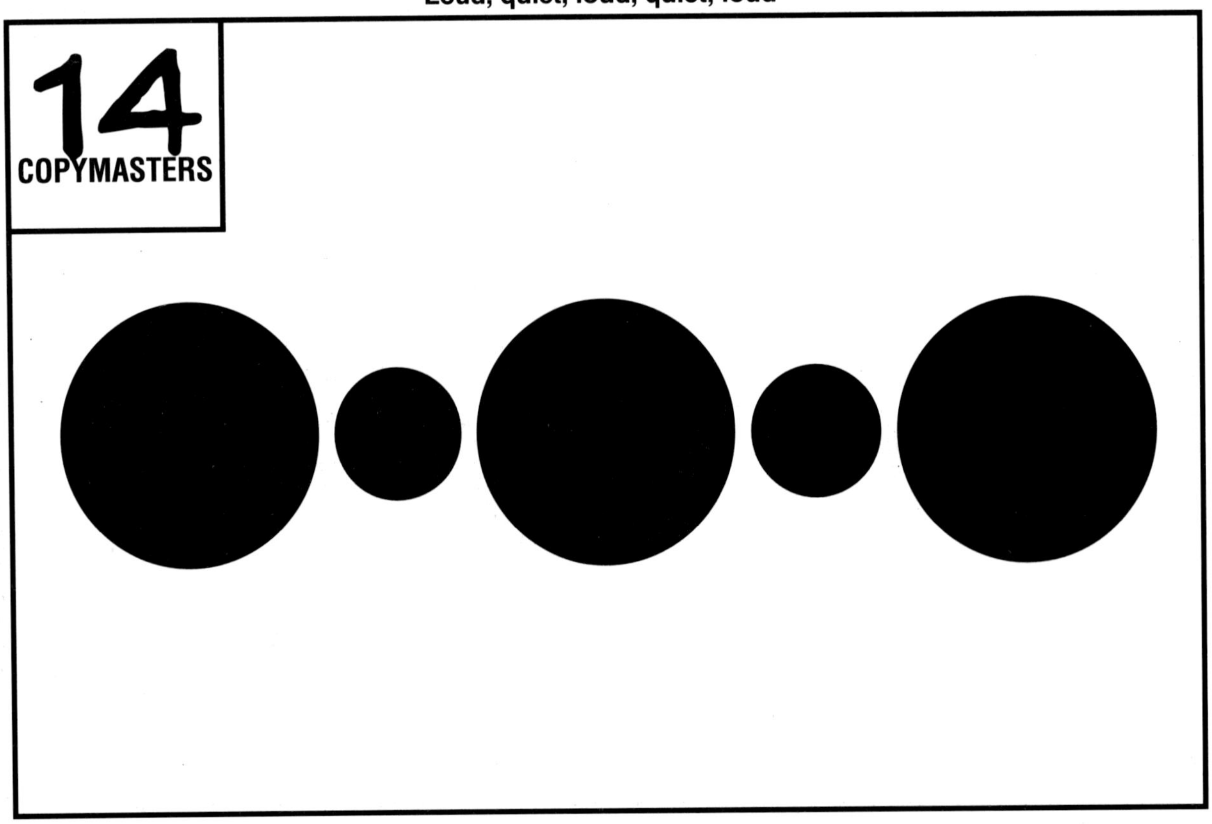

15

Quiet, quiet, quiet, quiet, loud

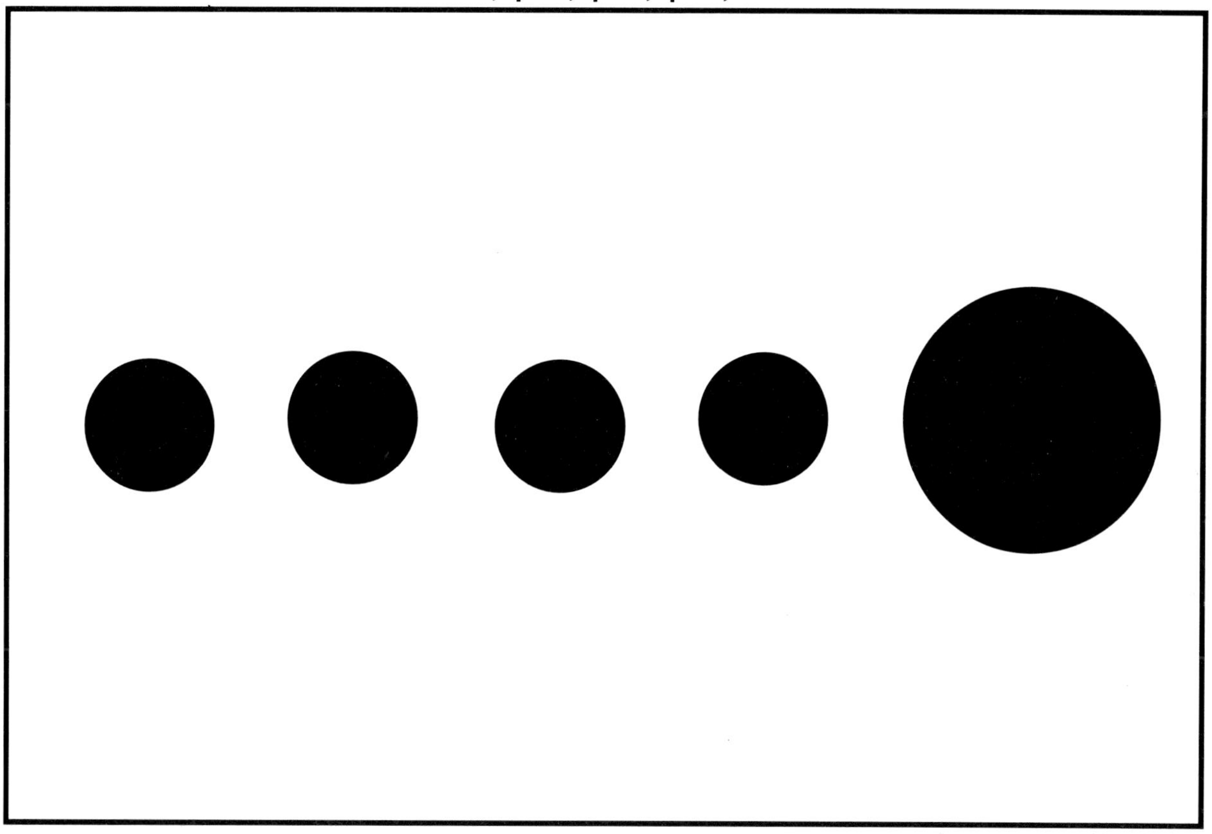

Quiet, loud, quiet

16 COPYMASTERS

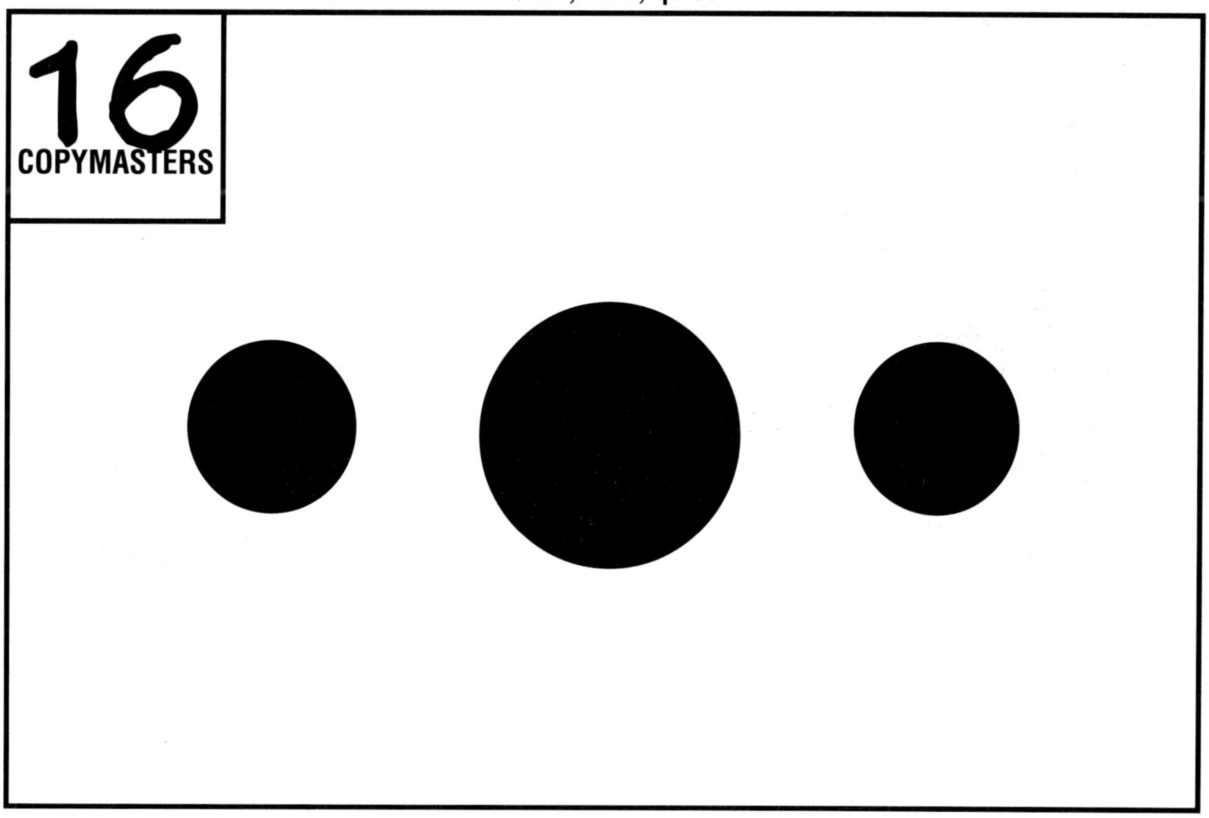

17

Loud, quiet, quiet, quiet, quiet, quiet,

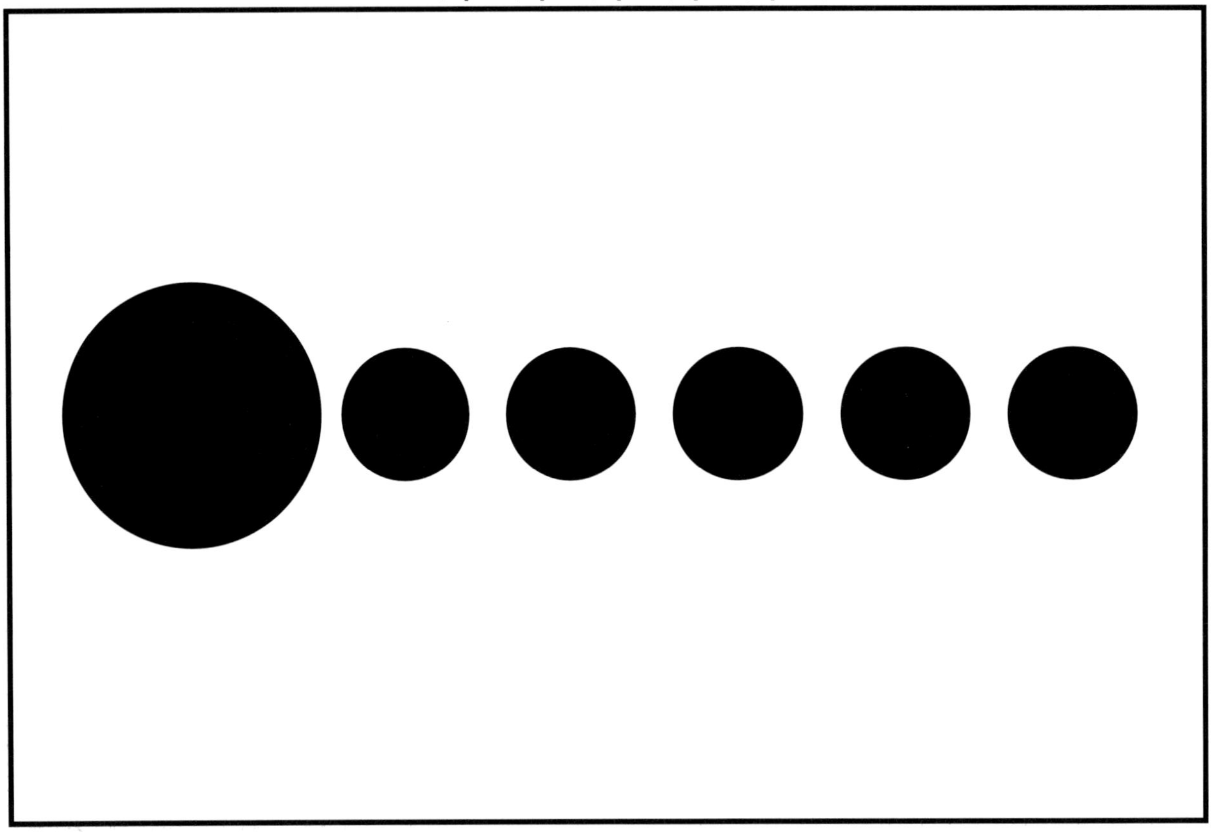

Gradually getting louder

18

COPYMASTERS

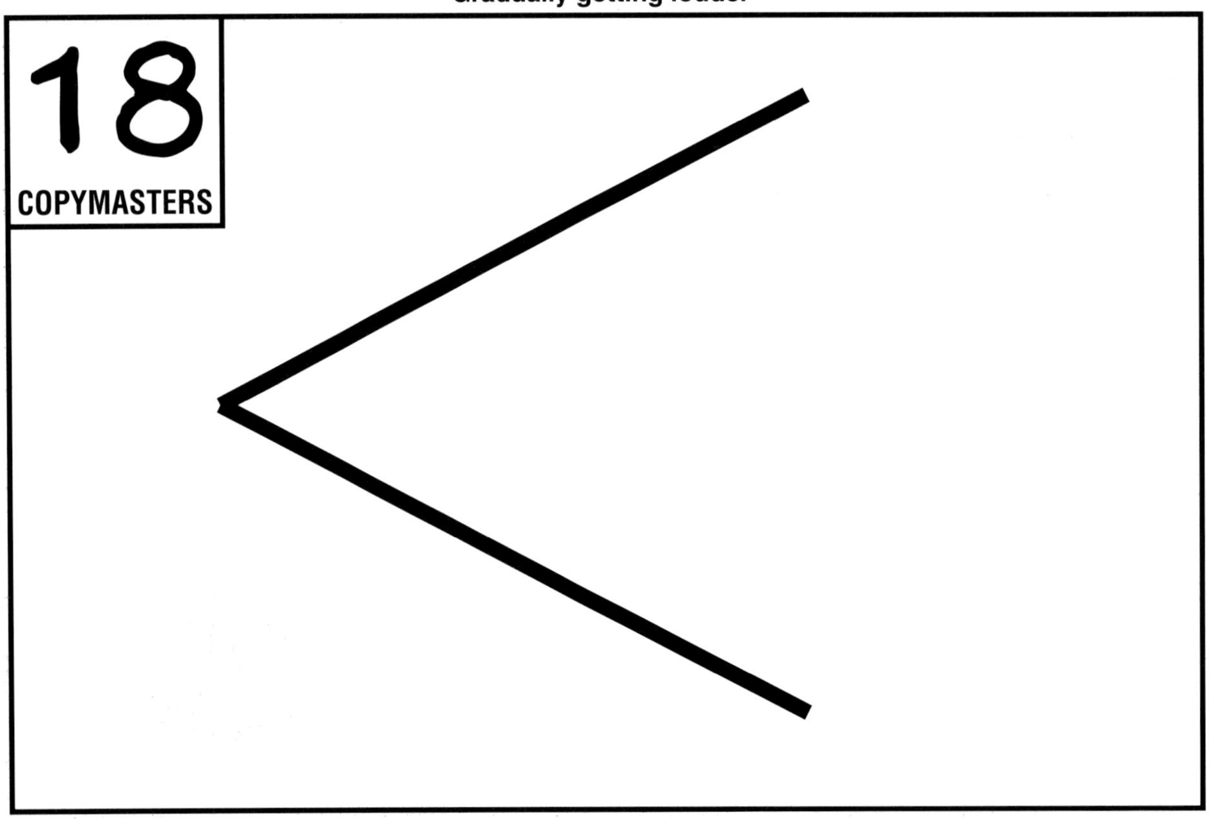

19

Gradually getting quieter

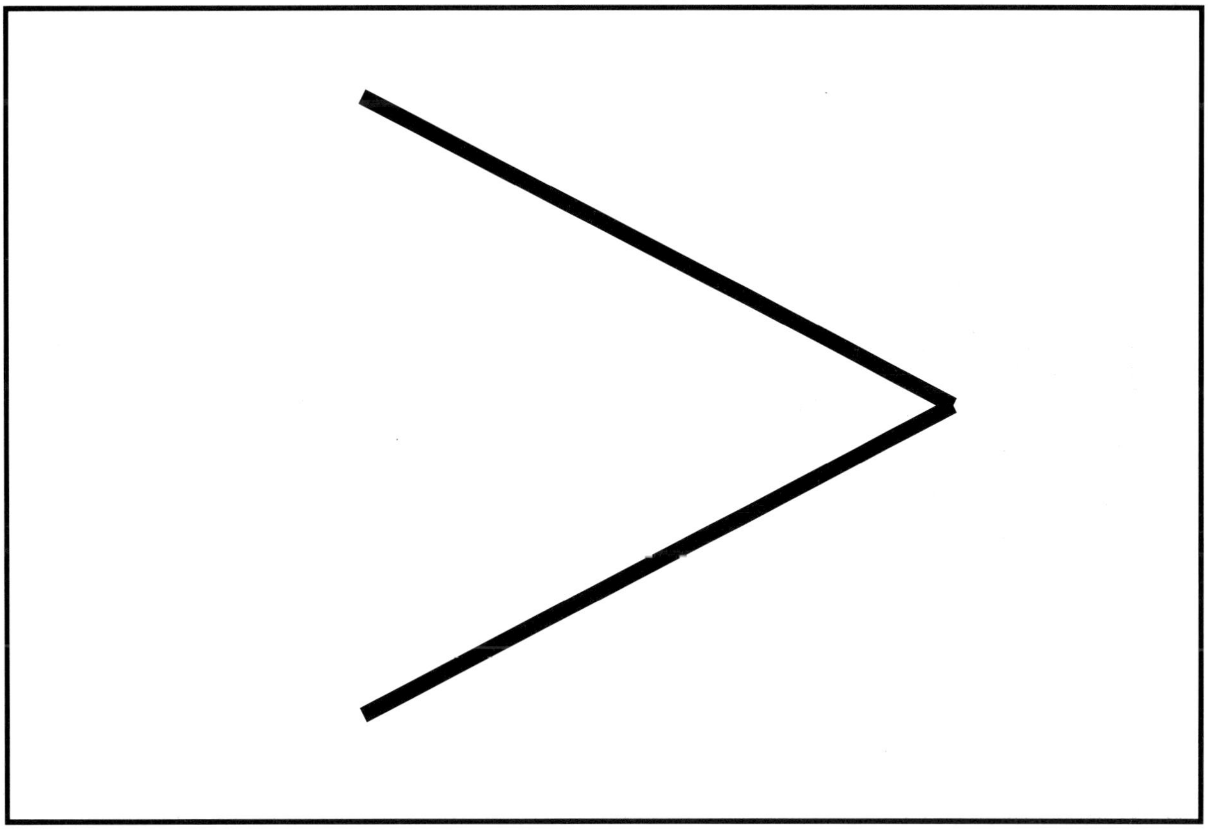

High, low

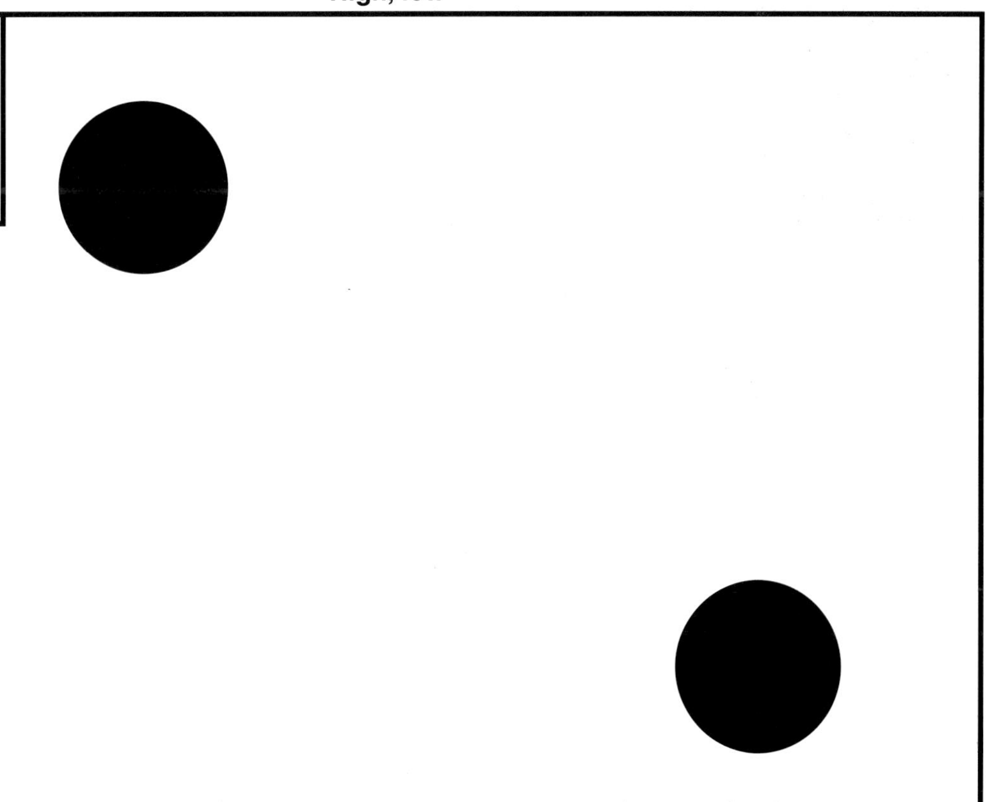

High, high, high

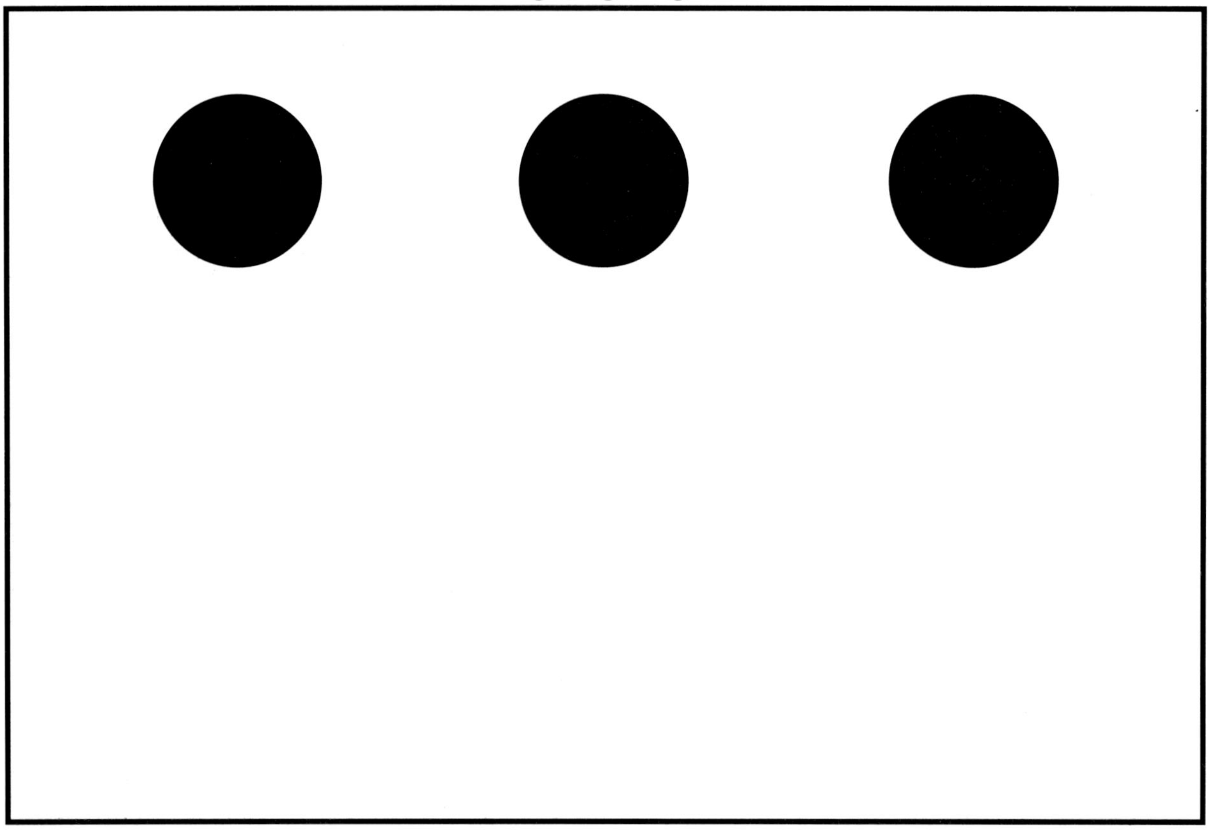

Low, low, low

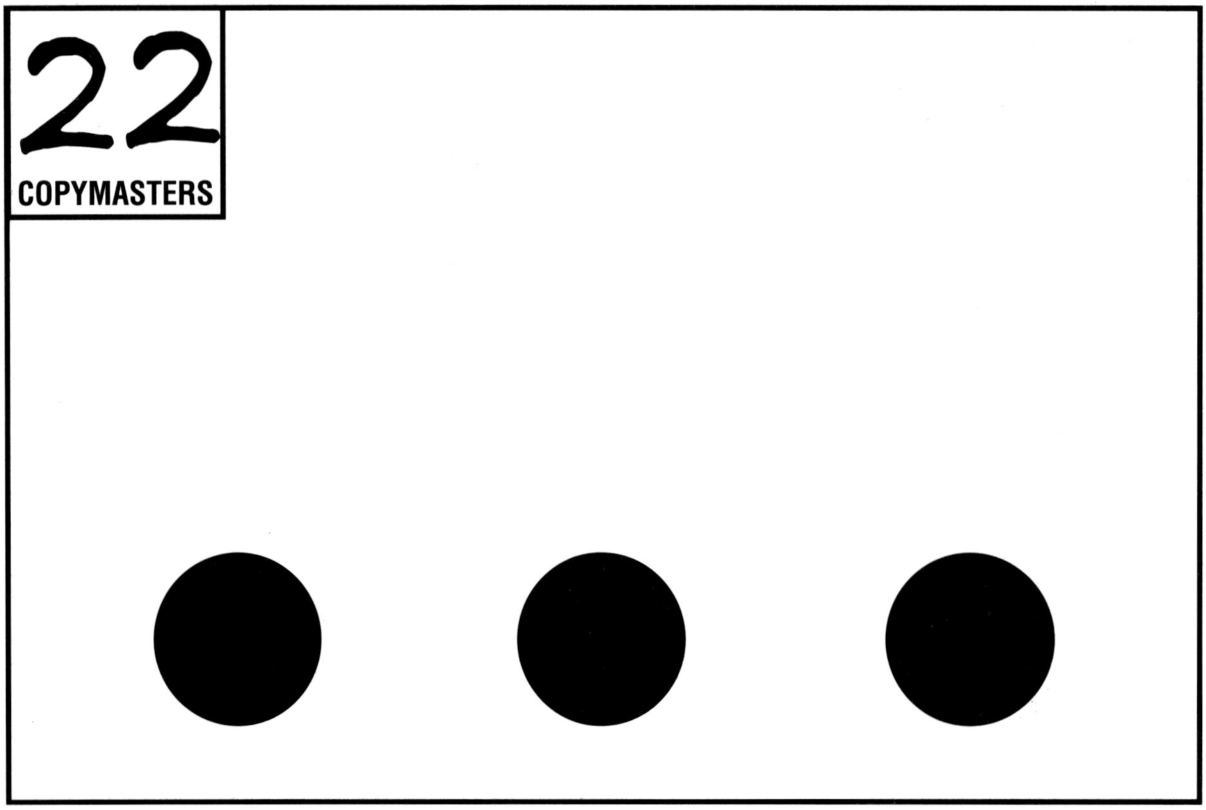

23

Low, high, low, high

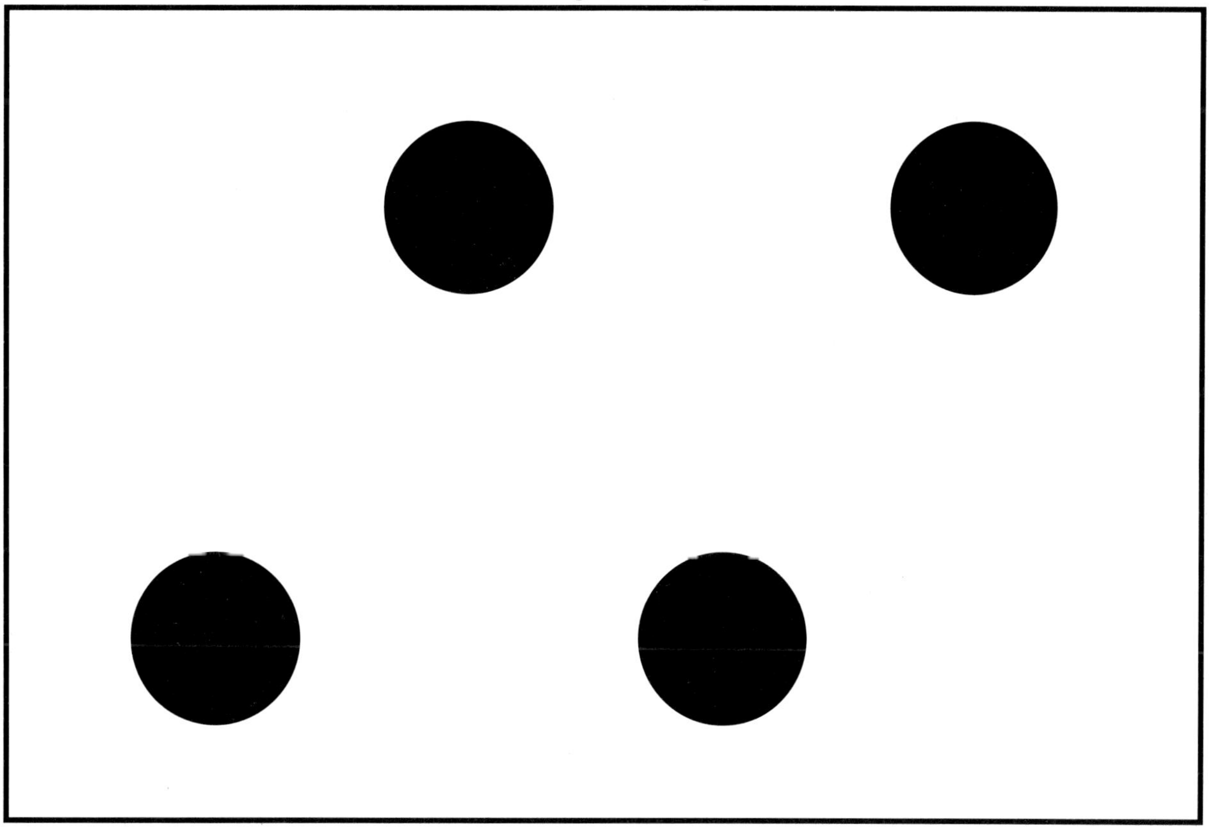

Low, high, high, low

24

COPYMASTERS

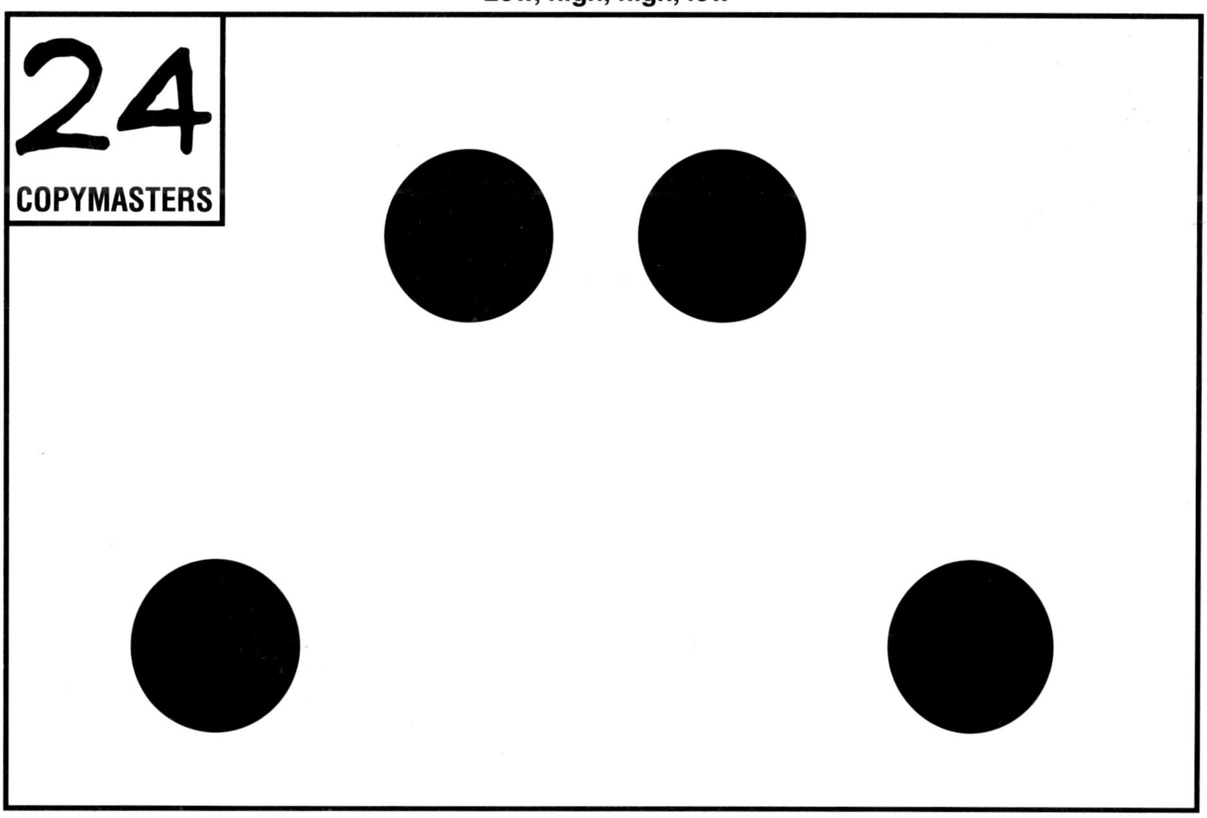

Notes played at the same pitch

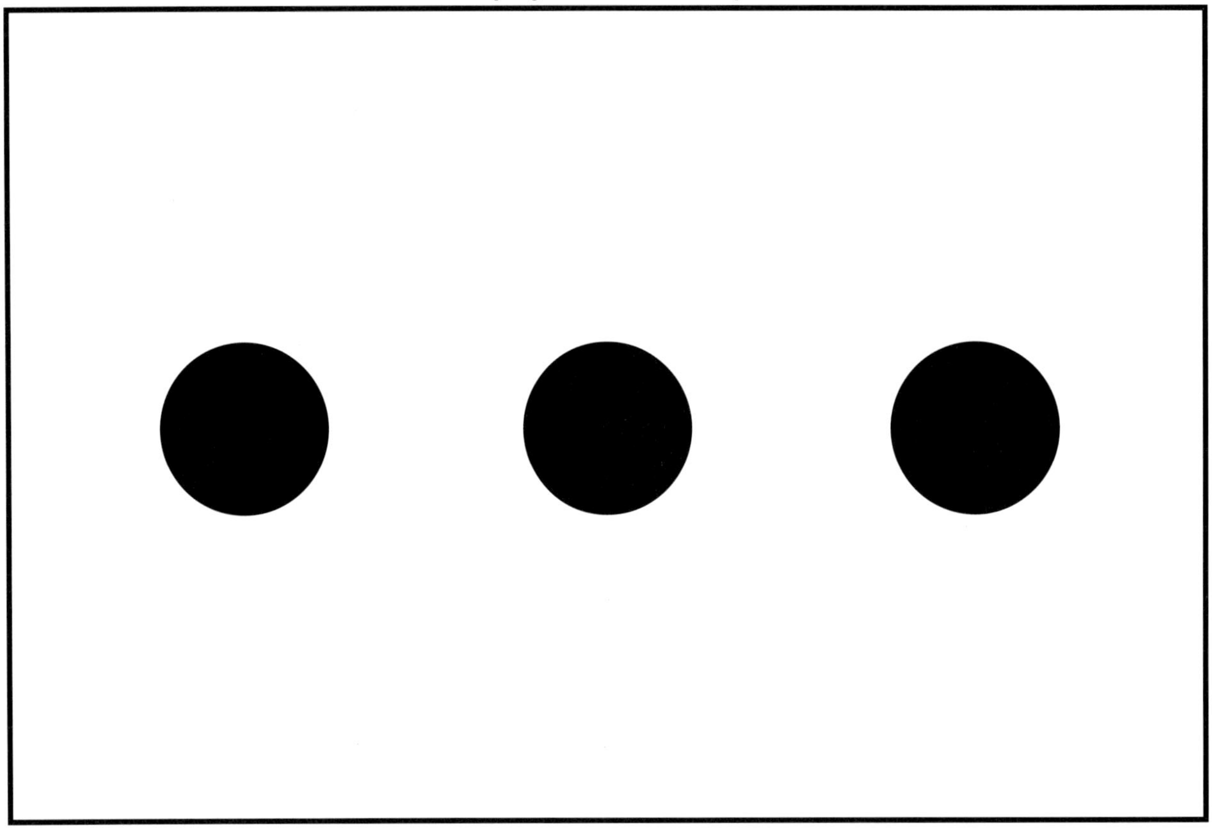

Loud sound

26

COPYMASTERS

Oh when the saints go marching in

I've been to Harlem

A ram sam sam

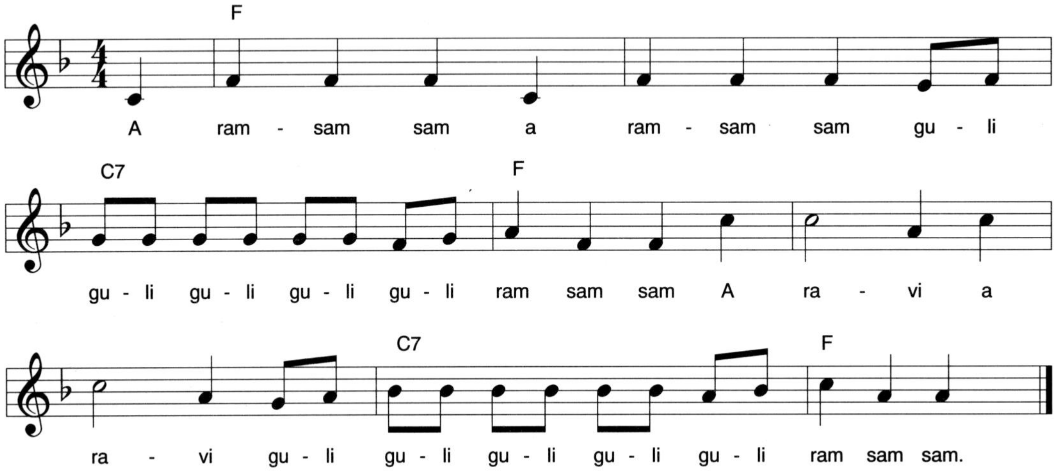

Tideo

Land of the silver birch

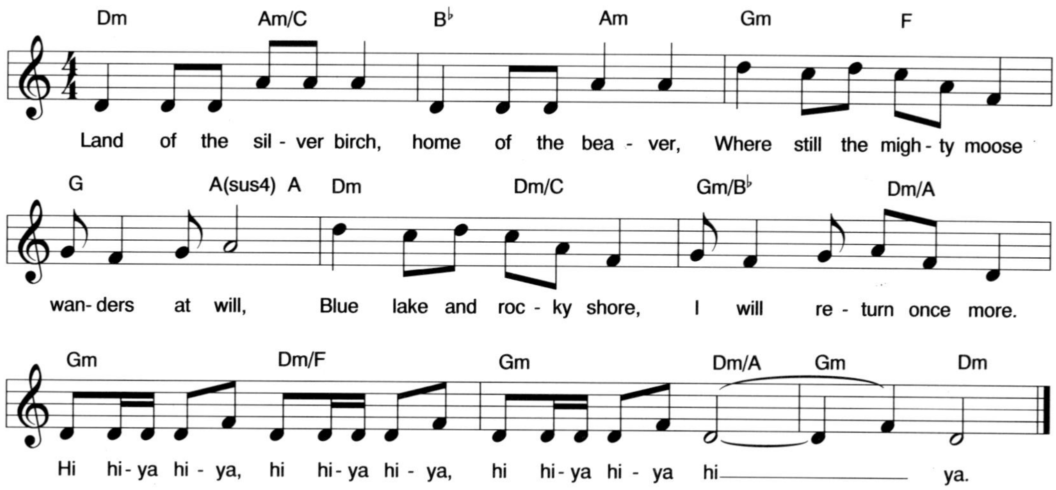

Doctor Foster

Round the circle

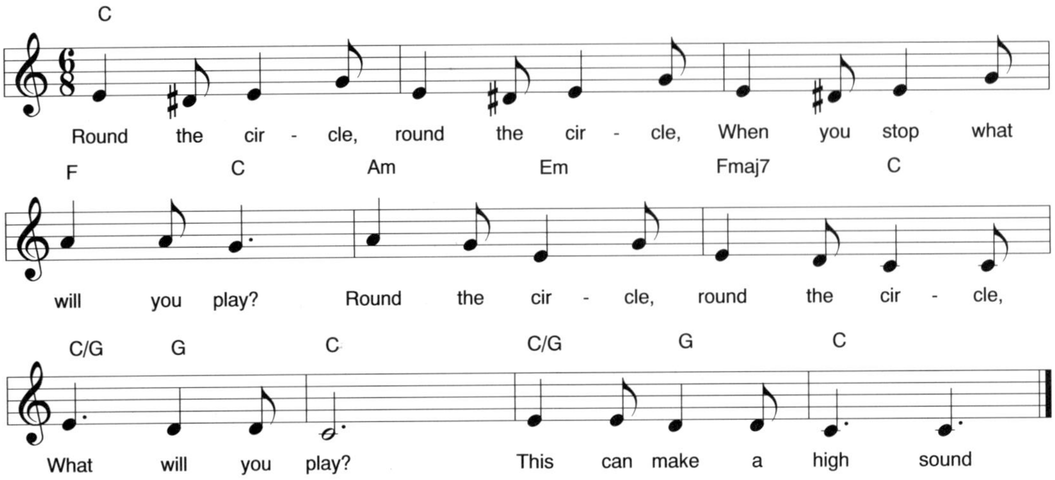

Luiseno Indian rain chant

Seasons

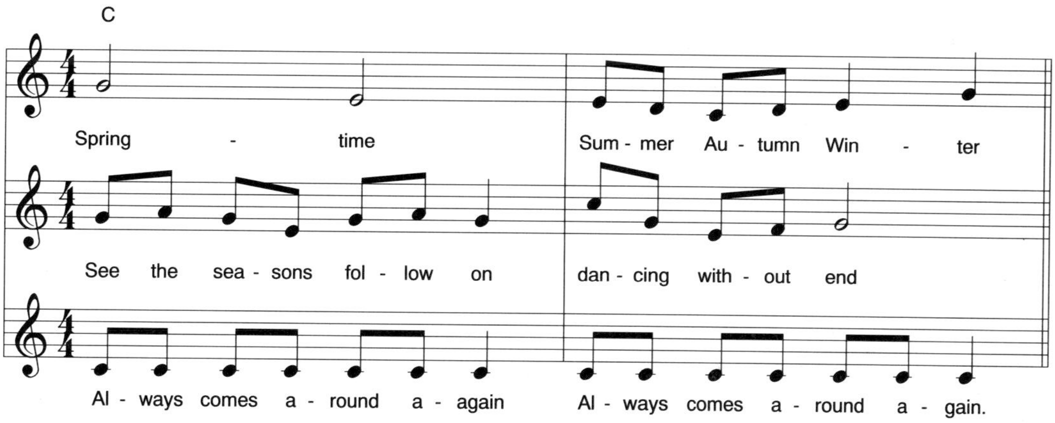

Fenyang flower drum song

Tshiyoyo

Mumma warrano

Way, way, the lion

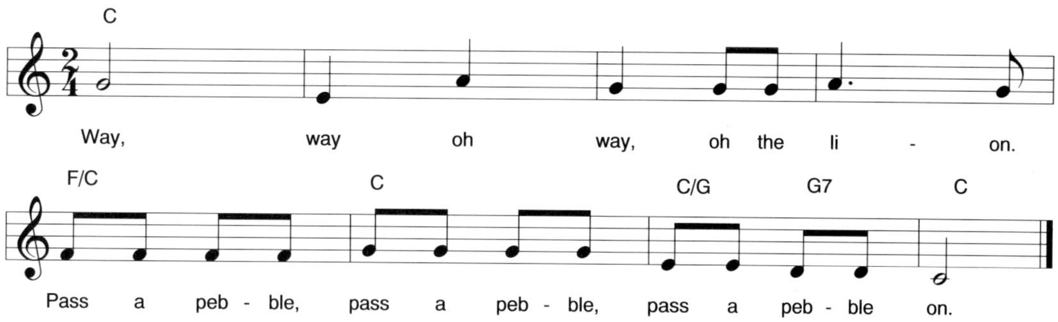

Kite

The old brass wagon

Hill an gully

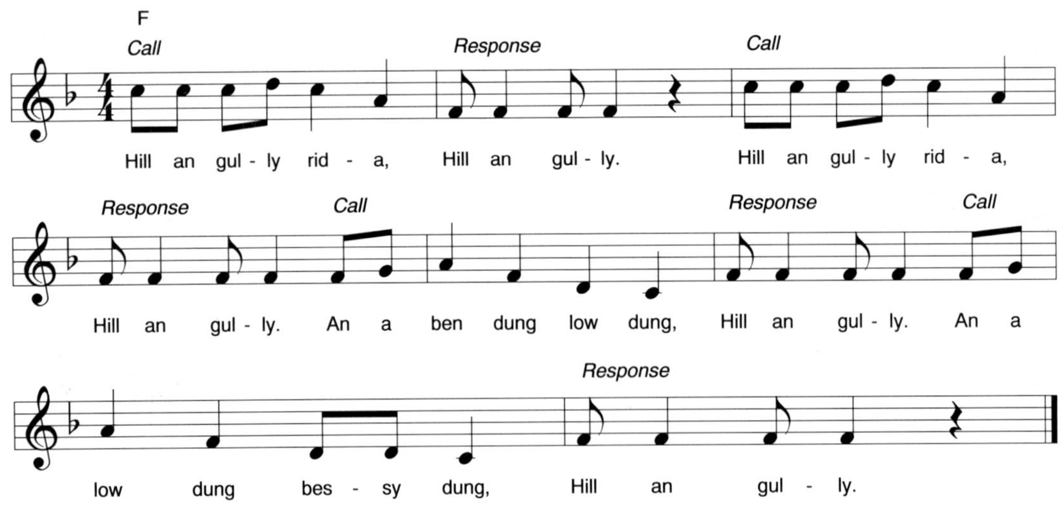

Riddle song

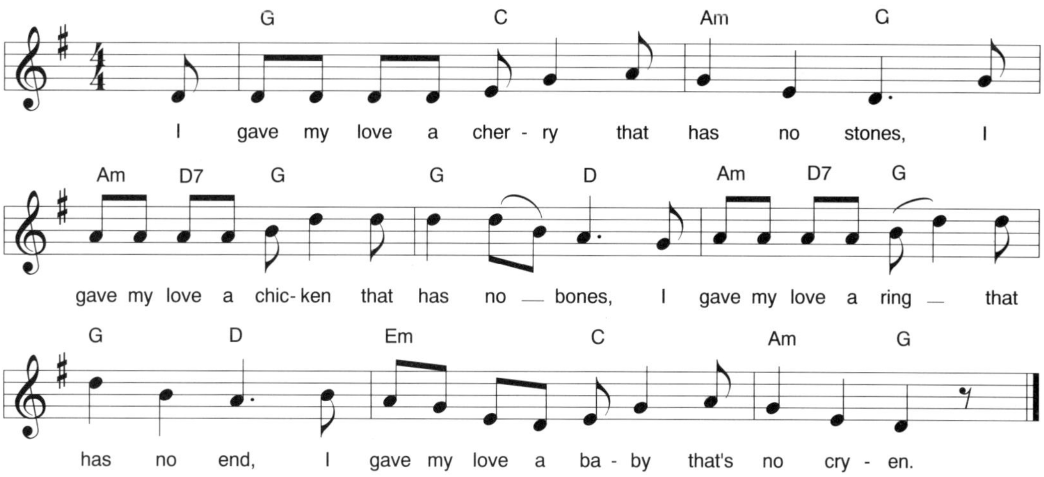

Everybody loves Saturday night

Dayenu

Hey ho, hey lo

The lemon tree

Listening materials

UNITS 1–2

Cassette 1

Side A)
Track
1 Signature tune
2 King Cotton
3 Shostakovitch's 5th symphony
4 The dance of nymphs and satyrs
5 Mosquito
6 Shine
7 When the saints go marching in
8 I've been to Harlem – *version 1*
9 A ram sam sam – *version 1*
10 Lincolnshire poacher

Side B)
Track
11 Blue Danube waltz
12 Silence is golden
13 I've been to Harlem – *version 2*
14 Kwacheri
15 Dont vient cela
16 A ram sam sam – *version 2*
17 I've been to Harlem – *version 3*
18 Tideo – *version 1*
19 Tideo – *version 2*
20 Tideo – *version 3*
21 Tideo – *version 4*
22 I've been to Harlem - *version 4*
23 Rise up o flame
24 Cantiga: como per sas culpas os omes
25 Land of the silver birch – *version 1*
26 Land of the silver birch – *version 2*
27 Land of the silver birch – *version 3*

Cassette 2

Side A)
Track
1 Signature tune
2 Doctor Foster
3 Kalinka
4 Round the circle
5 Sheherazade

Side B)
Track
6 Water in Yan river
7 Zuni Pueblo rainbow dance song
8 Listen to the sound of the gentle falling rain
9 Luiseno Indian rain chant
10 Rocks and pools

CD 1

Track
1 Signature tune
2 King Cotton
3 Shostakovitch's 5th symphony
4 The dance of nymphs and satyrs
5 Mosquito
6 Shine
7 When the saints go marching in
8 I've been to Harlem – *version 1*
9 A ram sam sam – *version 1*
10 Lincolnshire poacher
11 Blue Danube waltz
12 Silence is golden
13 I've been to Harlem – *version 2*
14 Kwacheri
15 Dont vient cela
16 A ram sam sam - *version 2*
17 I've been to Harlem – *version 3*
18 Tideo – *version 1*
19 Tideo – *version 2*
20 Tideo – *version 3*
21 Tideo – *version 4*
22 I've been to Harlem – *version 4*
23 Rise up o flame
24 Cantiga: como per sas culpas os omes
25 Land of the silver birch – *version 1*
26 Land of the silver birch – *version 2*
27 Land of the silver birch – *version 3*
28 Doctor Foster
29 Kalinka
30 Round the circle
31 Sheherazade
32 Water in Yan river
33 Zuni Pueblo rainbow dance song
34 Listen to the sound of the gentle falling rain
35 Luiseno Indian rain chant
36 Rocks and pools

UNITS 3–4

Cassette 3

Side A)
Track
1 Signature tune
2 Scherzo
3 Clock symphony
4 John Henry
5 The seasons – *version 1*
6 The seasons – *version 2*
7 The seasons – *version 3*
8 Fly, fly, fly
9 Yellow
10 End of summer
11 Summertime

Side B)
Track
12 The spring symphony
13 The rite of spring
14 On hearing the first cuckoo in spring
15 Fenyang flower drum song – *version 1*
16 Fenyang flower drum song – *version 2*
17 Antartica
18 Footsteps in the snow
19 Troika
20 Party tonight
21 Yu da ba jiao

Cassette 4

Side A)
Track
1 Signature tune
2 Dynamics
3 Tshiyoyo
4 Safari na muziki
5 Way way the lion – *version 1*
6 Way way the lion – *version 2*
7 Way way the lion – *version 3*

Side B)
Track
8 Mumma warrano – *version 1*
9 Mumma warrano – *version 2*
10 The organ concerto
11 I surrender
12 Samba triste
13 Pastoral symphony
14 A sea symphony

CD 2

Track
1 Signature tune
2 Scherzo
3 Clock symphony
4 John Henry
5 The seasons – *version 1*
6 The seasons – *version 2*
7 The seasons – *version 3*
8 Fly, fly, fly
9 Yellow
10 End of summer
11 Summertime
12 The spring symphony
13 The rite of spring
14 On hearing the first cuckoo in spring
15 Fenyang flower drum song – *version 1*
16 Fenyang flower drum song – *version 2*
17 Antartica
18 Footsteps in the snow
19 Troika
20 Party tonight
21 Yu da ba jiao
22 Dynamics
23 Tshiyoyo
24 Safari na muziki
25 Way way the lion – *version 1*
26 Way way the lion – *version 2*
27 Way way the lion – *version 3*
28 Mumma warrano – *version 1*
29 Mumma warrano – *version 2*
30 The organ concerto
31 I surrender
32 Samba triste
33 Pastoral symphony
34 A sea symphony

Cassette 5

Side A)
Track
1 Signature tune
2 Kite
3 The old brass wagon
4 Trisch trasch polka
5 Hill an gully rida
6 Canon
7 Mozart's 4th horn concerto
8 Beat feat
9 Changes
10 Boom chick a boom – *version 1*
11 Boom chick a boom – *version 2*
12 Boom chick a boom – *version 3*

Side B)
Track
13 Syrinx
14 Hiryu Sand An Gaeshi
15 Violin concerto – *extract 1*
16 Violin concerto – *extract 2*
17 Greensleeves to a ground – *extract 1*
18 Greensleeves to a ground – *extract 2*
19 The lark ascending
20 Knightsbridge march
21 The riddle song – *version 1*
22 The riddle song – *version 2*
23 The riddle song – *version 3*
24 Everybody loves saturday night – *version 1*
25 Everybody loves saturday night – *version 2*

Cassette 6

Side A)
Track
1 Signature tune
2 Dagbamba drummers: Tora
3 Independence song
4 Izithembifo zenkozi
5 Dance from Maramaros
6 Havah Nagilah
7 Dayenu
8 Lamenting song – *version 1*
9 Lamenting song – *version 2*

Side B)
Track
10 Is it clear or cloudy? – *version 1*
11 Is it clear or cloudy? – *version 2*
12 Hey ho, hey lo
13 The lemon tree
14 Sitar music
15 Tablar music
16 Raga bairagi todi
17 Soniaye ni soniaye

CD 3

Track
1 Signature tune
2 Kite
3 The old brass wagon
4 Trisch trasch polka
5 Hill an gully rida
6 Canon
7 Mozart's 4th horn concerto
8 Beat feat
9 Changes
10 Boom chick a boom – *version 1*
11 Boom chick a boom – *version 2*
12 Boom chick a boom – *version 3*
13 Syrinx
14 Hiryu Sand An Gaeshi
15 Violin concerto – *extract 1*
16 Violin concerto – *extract 2*
17 Greensleeves to a ground – *extract 1*
18 Greensleeves to a ground – *extract 2*
19 The lark ascending
20 Knightsbridge march
21 The riddle song – *version 1*
22 The riddle song – *version 2*
23 The riddle song – *version 3*
24 Everybody loves saturday night – *version 1*
25 Everybody loves saturday night – *version 2*
26 Dagbamba drummers: Tora
27 Independence song
28 Izithembifo zenkozi
29 Dance from Maramaros
30 Havah Nagilah
31 Dayenu
32 Lamenting song – *version 1*
33 Lamenting song – *version 2*
34 Is it clear or cloudy? – *version 1*
35 Is it clear or cloudy? – *version 2*
36 Hey ho, hey lo
37 The lemon tree
38 Sitar music
39 Tablar music
40 Raga bairagi todi
41 Soniaye ni soniaye

Cross-curricular links

Opportunities exist to link music to learning in other subjects. These have been highlighted throughout the text and have been listed below as an aid to planning.

Art

Unit 2, page 37
Draw, paint, use pastels and try printing from and painting string to make patterns of contoured lines.

Unit 3, page 59
Look at paintings related to the seasons of the year e.g. for winter, Monet's 'Winter in Vetheuil', 'Break up of ice, Lavercourt', 'Sunshine and snow, Lavercourt', and Breugel the Elder's 'Hunters in the snow'. For autumn, 'Autumn leaves', by John Everett Millais. For summer, Seurat's 'The bather' and 'Sunday afternoon on the Grand Jette'. For spring, 'Early spring', by John William Inchbold, or 'Spring at Giverny', by Monet.

Unit 3, page 59
Encourage the children to draw/paint pictures to go with the listening extracts or their own compositions.

Science and Technology

Unit 2, page 37
Create echo sounds by beating boxes. Investigate how the volume of the box affects the sound produced. Find areas of the school where vocal echo sounds can be made e.g. gym, empty classroom. Investigate the differences between areas where the sound can be produced and where it cannot.

Unit 2, page 40
Make instruments to measure weather phenomena e.g. rain guage, wind meter. Write weather reports and try predicting the weather for the following day/week.

Dance

Unit 2, page 49
Create movements to the children's composition.

Untuned percussion instruments

Shaking and scraping instruments

Metal instruments

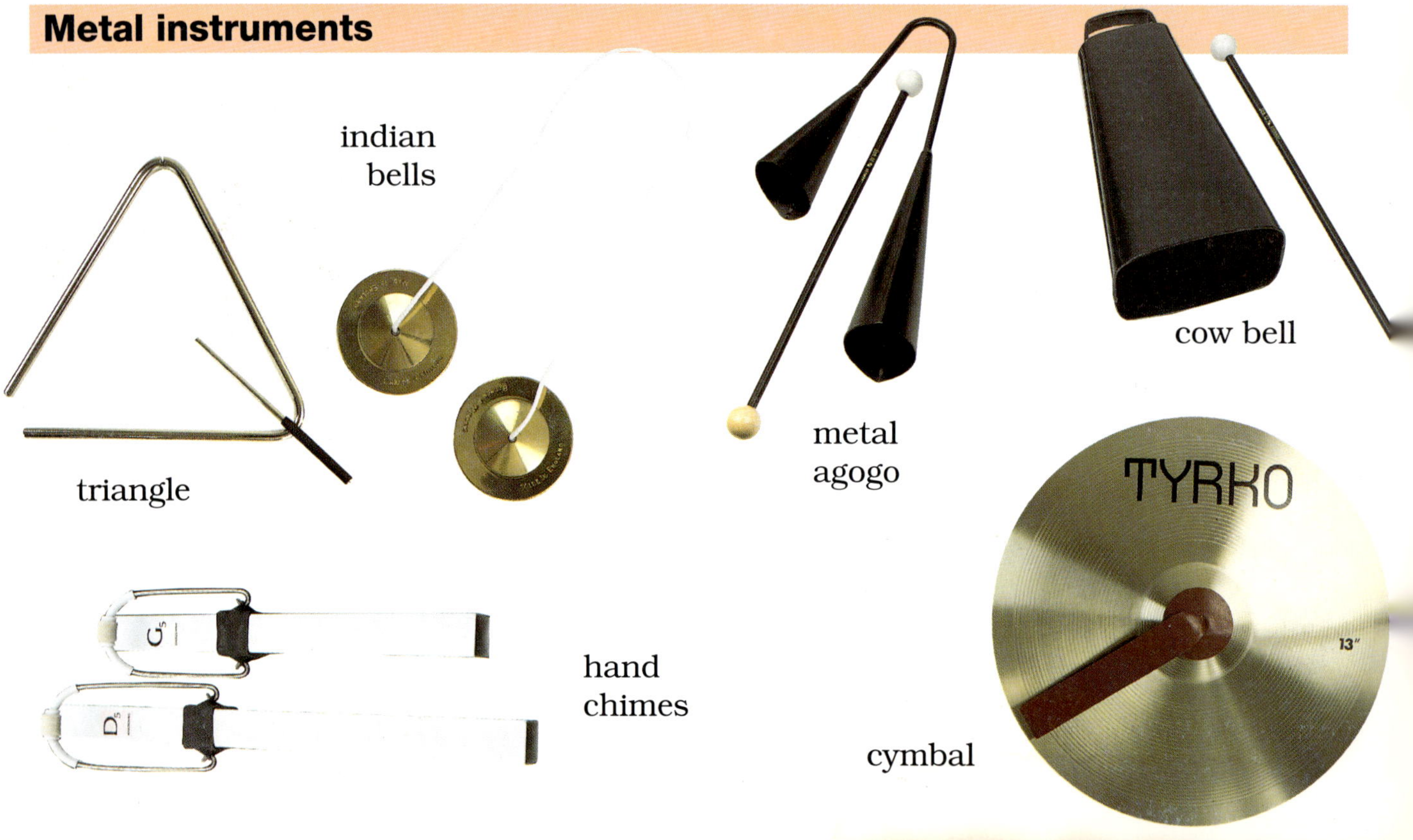

Wooden instruments

slit drum

claves

wood-block

wood-block

Skin instruments

tambourine

tambour

bongos

Tuned percussion instruments

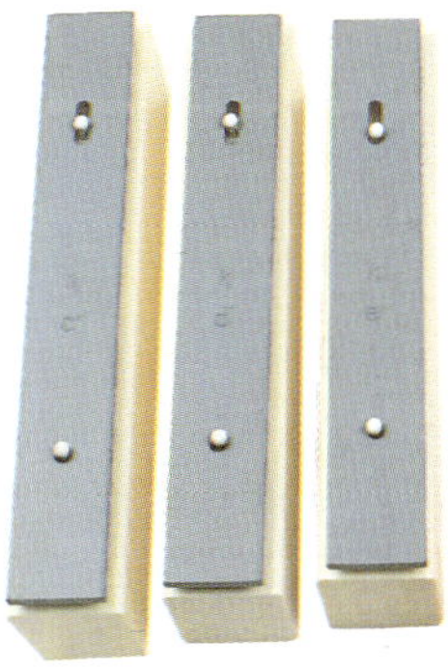
metal chime bars

metallophone

wooden chime bars

glockenspiel

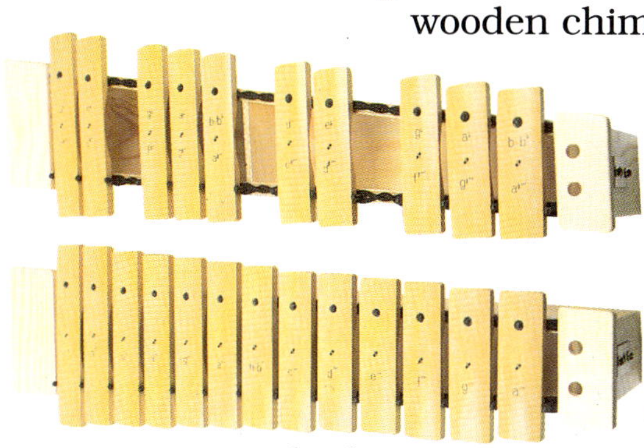
xylophone

A guide to assessment

STUDENT NAME

	Unit 1	Unit 2	Unit 3	Unit 4	Unit 5	Unit 6
PERFORMING	maintain a steady beat with control using a variety of body percussion sounds and percussion instruments accurately perform rhythm patterns grouped in twos, threes and fours on a variety of sound sources sing a variety of songs perform accompaniment patterns from rhythm notations sing rounds in two parts	sing songs play rhythmic and melodic patterns with control	explore and find different ways of creating a variety of sounds with percussion instruments and voices perform a round with two parts/groups sing a variety of songs including material from other cultures perform a simple rhythm pattern as an accompaniment to a song perform a drone	control loud and quiet sounds on a variety of sound sources perform loud and quiet sounds in response to graphic symbols on a variety of sound sources perform a variety of songs perform simple accompaniment patterns with a song perform loud/quiet in response to a given instruction	perform high and low accurately in response to symbols sing songs combine rhythm and pitch add a drone as an accompaniment to a song	perform a steady beat on body percussion, responding to a quickening tempo perform a vocal chant at different speeds maintaining control sing a variety of songs add simple accompaniment patterns to songs
COMPOSING		create sound pieces using words and poems as stimuli create a piece with ABA structure create a sound piece that contains pitched sounds and unpitched sounds create a piece of music that communicates a particular effect	create a sequence of sounds using a specific timbre create a sound sequence that evokes the mood of a given stimulus by using an appropriate timbre use words as a stimulus for creating a sound sequence use and create poems as stimuli for composing create a graphic score of their own music		create simple pitch sequences create symbols that represent different pitches	create a rhythm pattern based on words create a melody from a given sequence of notes explore sounds in the environment and use them as a stimulus to create a sound piece
LISTENING	recognise the way beats are grouped by listening recognise an ostinato pattern recognise a drone respond through movement to a part of a round	differentiate between instruments that can play pitch and those that cannot recognise music that has ABA structure	listen to and answer questions about sound recognise and name different timbres identify sounds/ instruments and how they are used to communicate an effect	identify loud/quiet sounds played on percussion instruments record graphically loud/quiet, louder/quieter sounds from an extract of music identify loud/quiet music when listening	respond to high and low sounds aurally recognise pitch moving up or down a step	respond through movement to different tempos in music identify music with and without melody listen to and identify sounds in the local environment
APPRAISING		talk about and express opinions about music they and others have created talk about different sounds/timbres that percussion instruments make	work cooperatively as a member of a group talk about, and order, separate sound sequences into a structured composition listen to extracts of music and talk about sounds/effects created	talk about sounds they make and listen to their dynamic (loud/quiet) level discuss which instruments are best for loud sounds and which for quiet discuss and share ideas about arranging an accompaniment for a song	talk about the way to communicate a sound to someone else	listen to extracts of music and express ideas and opinions talk about the differences between music from different countries talk about music they heard, referring to words they have understood e.g. 'drone', 'ostinato'

Introduced to skill | Has attained skill | Confident in using skill

Glossary

Accompaniment: Sounds added to a song, melody, poem, or story.

ABA structure: This is a musical structure which is composed of three parts, where the first and third parts are the same and the middle part is different.

Body percussion: clapping hands, rubbing hands, finger tapping, clicking fingers, patting shoulders, patting knees, stamping/sliding feet

Chromatic instruments: These are tuned instruments e.g. glockenspiels, xylophones etc. that have sharps # and flats ♭. They have an additional row of notes which equate to the black notes on a piano or electronic keyboard.

Contour: The shape of a melody – the way that it moves upwards and downwards. See also Melody.

Drone: The same note or notes played constantly.

Glissando: Sliding a beater across the xylophone/metallophone/glockenspiel bars in one sweeping movement.

Graphic score: A way of fixing musical sounds on paper by representing them with any sign, symbol, shape or words that communicate the composer's intentions.

Grid: An accessible and clear way of displaying and recording notation; an easy device for performing from.

Improvise: Making up music 'on the spot'.

Melody: A sequence of notes (pitches) that are structured in such a way as to form a tune e.g. moving upwards/downwards by step/leap, or repeating notes.

Musical elements: These are key concepts in music.

- **Pitch** – high and low sounds; sounds moving upwards and downwards by steps and leaps; letter names for pitches e.g. D and A
- **Duration** – rhythm patterns; beats grouped in twos, threes and fours
- **Dynamics** – different levels of volume – loud and quiet; getting gradually louder/quieter
- **Tempo** – different speeds – fast and slow; getting gradually faster/slower
- **Timbre** – the personality of a sound; how one sound differs from another
- **Texture** – layers of sounds e.g. building up rhythm patterns; adding accompaniments to songs
- **Structure** – the overall shape/form of music (see also ABA structure and rondo)

Notation: Any word, picture, or symbol which is used to represent sounds.

Ostinato: A short rhythmic or melodic pattern that is repeated throughout a piece or a part of a piece.

Pentatonic scale: A scale that consists of 5 different notes

Phrase: A musical sentence

Raga: The name given to the structure of Indian scales

Rhythm pattern: A pattern of long and short sounds and silences. Rhythm differs from steady beat: steady beat is usually made up of equal sounds, like a heart-beat or a ticking clock, whereas rhythm sounds may be differently spaced and have different lengths.

Rondo: A piece of music in which one section (A) keeps returning after new sections (B/C etc.) have been played e.g. ABACADA.

Steady beat: The underlying beat in a piece of music or poetry. The beat is steady, equal and constant.

Symbol: The picture, shape, or word chosen to represent a given sound.

Time names: Spoken syllables can be used to help the accurate performance of rhythm patterns:

taa ta-tay saa

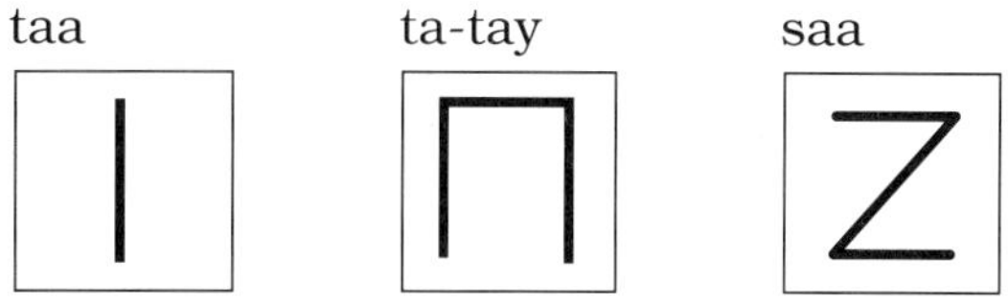

Trill: A rapid movement between two notes, or sounds, on an instrument.

Tuned percussion instruments: Percussion instruments that can play a melody/tune as well as a rhythm e.g. xylophone, glockenspiel etc.

Untuned percussion instruments: Percussion instruments that can play only rhythm and not melody/tune e.g. wood-block, drum etc.

Vocal sounds: tongue clicking; making sounds with parts of the mouth – 'hmm', 'ooh', 'ah'; phonic sounds e.g. 'ttt', 'shh', 'rrr' etc.

Acknowledgements

"SHINE" Music by Ford T Dabney and words by Cecil Mack and Lew Brown © 1924, Shapiro Bernstein and Co Inc, USA
Reproduced by permission of EMI Music Publishing Ltd, LondonWC2H OEA

'I've been to Harlem' and 'A ram sam sam' for Marta Nemesszeghy's children's song book by Deanna Hoermann

'Breezes are blowing', 'End of Summer', 'Zulu Game Song', 'Everybody loves Saturday night', 'Hey ho, hey lo', 'Dayenu', Silver Burdett Ginn

'The organ concerto', by Poulenc – DECCA 425 627-2; played by the Academy of St Martin in the Fields; Iona Brown (opening only)

'Samba triste', from 'Acoustic colours – The famous guitars', played by Baden Powell, Polygram UK

Vaughan Williams 'A sea symphony'
℗1989 The copyright on this recording is owned by EMI Records Ltd

Johann Strauss II 'Tritsch-Tratsch Polka'
℗1961 The copyright in this recording is owned by EMI Records Limited

Boom Chick a boom
'Sing for pleasure', 25 Fyerning Lane, Ingatestone, Essex, CM4 ODD

'Dance from Maramaros' and Lamenting song' Ryko Disc UK Ltd.

'Havah Nagilah' from Traditional Jewish melodies – Benedict Silberman, orchestra and chorus. Legacy International CD 395, co-produced by SISU Home Entertainments Inc. Under licence from TKO Records, Great Britain

Ralph Vaughan Williams Symphony no.7 'Sinfonia Antartica', Andre Previn and the London Symphony Orchestra on RCA Victor Gold Seal Series, RCA Corporation. Published by Oxford University Press

'John Henry' by Copland
SONY; performed by the London Symphony Orchestra, conducted by A. Copland.
Published by Boosey and Hawkes

'The rite of spring' by Stravinsky Eliahu Inbal and the Philharmonica Orchestra on Teldec.
© 1990, 1991 by Teldec Classics International GMBH
A Time Warner company
Published by Boosey and Hawkes

'Syrinx' by Debussy, from 'Claire de Lune', played by James Galway, Marisa Robles and the Chamber Youth Orchestra. RCA copyright, 1986, Ariola International, printed in West Germany, RCA Corporation. Red Seal digital series.

'Dont vient cela' by Tielman Susato from 'Pastyme with Good Companye', Cantoris Griffin CRCD2365. Published by Cantoris Griffin, specialists in recorded early music, Church House, St. Mary's Gate, 96 Church Street, Lancaster LA1 1TD

Britten 'A Spring Symphony', performed by the Orchestra and Chorus of the Royal Opera House (Cat No. 425 153-2), The Decca Record Company Limited

Published by Boosey and Hawkes.

'Summertime' from 'Porgy and Bess' by George Gershwin, sung by Lesley Garrett and accompanied by The Philharmonia Orchestra, conducted by Ivor Bolton on CD entitled 'Prima Donna',
© 1992 Silva Screen Records Ltd

'The Lincolnshire Poacher'played by the CWS (Glasgow) Band from 'The Pioneers March'. Kirklees Music

'Safari Na Muziki' by Hukwe Zawose, Triple Earth Music

'Fenyang Flower Drum Song' by Gaik See Chew.

'Silence is Golden' by The Tremeloes © Castle Communications PLC.

Every effort has been made to trace all the copyright holders but if any have been inadvertently overlooked the publisher will be pleased to make the necessary arrangement at the first opportunity.